ONCE UPON A DREAM

Verses In Moonlight

Edited By Lynsey Evans

First published in Great Britain in 2024 by:

YoungWriters
Est. 1991

Young Writers
Remus House
Coltsfoot Drive
Peterborough
PE2 9BF
Telephone: 01733 890066
Website: www.youngwriters.co.uk

All Rights Reserved
Book Design by Ashley Janson
© Copyright Contributors 2024
Softback ISBN 978-1-83565-738-6
Printed and bound in the UK by BookPrintingUK
Website: www.bookprintinguk.com
YB0604F

FOREWORD

Welcome Reader, to a world of dreams.

For Young Writers' latest competition, we asked our writers to dig deep into their imagination and create a poem that paints a picture of what they dream of, whether it's a make-believe world full of wonder or their aspirations for the future.

The result is this collection of fantastic poetic verse that covers a whole host of different topics. Let your mind fly away with the fairies to explore the sweet joy of candy lands, join in with a game of fantasy football, or you may even catch a glimpse of a unicorn or another mythical creature. Beware though, because even dreamland has dark corners, so you may turn a page and walk into a nightmare!

Whereas the majority of our writers chose to stick to a free verse style, others gave themselves the challenge of other techniques such as acrostics and rhyming couplets. We also gave the writers the option to compose their ideas in a story, so watch out for those narrative pieces too!

Each piece in this collection shows the writers' dedication and imagination – we truly believe that seeing their work in print gives them a well-deserved boost of pride, and inspires them to keep writing, so we hope to see more of their work in the future!

CONTENTS

Ashley Academy, South Shields

Aaleyah Mahmud (11)	1
Kate Newton (10)	2
Gracie-Mae Robb (10)	4
Delta Miller (8)	5
Hayley Airey (10)	6
Isaac Dunlop (8)	7
Alicia Waite (9)	8
Freja Best (10)	9
Harlo-Rose Brown (11)	10
Dominic Burns (8)	11
Enya-Rose Fisher (10)	12
Ethan Mukuruva (10)	13
Kiam Salik (8)	14
Finley Errington (10)	15
Eva Swinbanks (9)	16
Isla Rothery (11)	17
Aliza Wilson (7)	18
Jasmine Hobbs (8)	19
Zoe Harvey (9)	20
Matilda Envy (8)	21
Peyton Elliott (8)	22
Bobbi Price (10)	23
Isla Forrester (9)	24
Eden Lodge (11)	25
Savannah Ruane (10)	26
Bella (8)	27
Skyler Fisher (8)	28
Isabel Bates (9)	29
Dylan Yeeles (9)	30
Theo Walker (7)	31

Chagford CE Primary School, Chagford

Evan Kempe (10)	32
Frida Lawrence (11)	33

Grace Mary Primary School, Oldbury

Grace Adebogun (9)	34
Alicia Westwood (9)	37
Willow Cains (8)	38
Kellie Brittain (9)	40
Carter Babington (9)	42
Ezra Agbebi (9)	44
Ezzmai Lunn (9)	46
Piper Bates (9)	48
Esther Parkes (9)	50
Elrad Agbebi (8)	51
Kavya Shah (8)	52
Evelyna Welsh (8)	54
Alliyah Hall (9)	55
Jovan Sandhu (9)	56
Danyal Shah (9)	57
Grace Smith (9)	58
Frankie Byrne (9)	59
Ruby Cheshire (8)	60
Angel Davis (9)	61
Olivia Woolley (9)	62
Evie-Mai Arnold (8)	63
Skylar-Rose Hayes (9)	64
Minnie Flavell (9)	65
Penelope Lee Williams (9)	66
Kobe Bellfield-Shearwood (9)	67
Ismail Ajmal (9)	68

Hale Preparatory School, Hale

Pearse Sheehy (11)	69
Ela Walshaw (11)	70
Esther Eckersley (11)	71

Harris Primary Academy Chafford Hundred, Grays

Idil Tunc (11)	72
Kouami Zewu-Manscour (11)	73
Ayan Hussain (11)	74
Dovydas Dula (11)	75
Saanvi Bolisetty (10)	76
Emily Georgieva (10)	77
Lily Adedipe (11)	78
Helena Rose (11)	79
Timas Miknevicius (10)	80
Joannabel Emma Eshun (11)	81
Sophie Chapman (11)	82
Edwin Kokogho (10)	83

Holsworthy CE Primary School, Holsworthy

Melody Nicholls (8)	84
Elsie Jourdain (10)	85
Holly-Ann Neale (9)	86
Isabelle Atkins (9)	87
Chloe Stacey (9)	88
Hannah Cholwill (10)	89
Erin Murdock (8)	90
Thomas Hurst (7)	91
Ellie Plumb (7)	92
Isabella Loach (8)	93
Leyla Prouse (9)	94
Beth Hammond (9)	95
Amelia Matthews (8)	96
Darina Tyschenko (8)	97
Willow Read (9)	98

James Wolfe Primary School Upper Campus, London

Sochi Agulanna (9)	99
Zella Mohammed Ziad (10)	100
Rachael Skipper (10)	101
Salimatu Bibah (10)	102
Zoe Liscovsky Colussi (10)	103
Ella Dhue (9)	104
Olivia Ng (9)	105

Manorfield CE Primary School, Stoney Stanton

Luke Ray (9)	106
Mollie Clarke (9)	107
Isabelle Fowkes (9)	108
Freddie Hayward (9)	110
Oscar Roach (8)	111
Lexi-Rae Joyce (9)	112
Theodore Needham (9)	113
Grayson Greenland (9)	114
Nicolas Regena (9)	115
Millie Fry (9)	116
AJ Taylor (9)	117
Oliver Grant (9)	118
Eliza Bennett (9)	119
Milen Rowe (8)	120
Honey Seaton (9)	121
Seth Currie (9)	122
Olly Brewin (8)	123
Lewis Cameron Breach (8)	124
Leila Dennis (9)	125
Rihan Stokes (9)	126
Jack Siddall (9)	127
Isla Rouse (9)	128
Erin Chambers (8)	129
Lila Abell (9)	130
Eden Jones (10)	131
Eva Rose Major (8)	132
Alfie Beckman (9)	133
Millie Cassell (9)	134
Noah Smith (9)	135
Ronnie Willows (9)	136

Artjoms Trifonovs (9)	137
Sebby Jones (9)	138
Sebastian Wegerif (9)	139
Lewis Sterland (8)	140
Franklin Knight (8)	141
Max Holmes (9)	142
Alaya Cherry (9)	143
Arrabella Rose Lee-Fowler (9)	144
Tom Farrell (9)	145
Casper White (9)	146
James Pickering (9)	147
James Heptinstall (9)	148
Myla Shilcock (8)	149
Kelly Wassell (9)	150
Jacob Grant (9)	151
Ayesha Stratton (9)	152
Samuel Savage (9)	153
Elliott Booth (9)	154
Lily Moulin (9)	155
Connie Law (9)	156
Isla Rae Warner (9)	157
Rardya Babu (8)	158
Evelyn Bostock (9)	159
Delaney Keeler (9)	160
Max Chapman (9)	161
Zachary Blockley (8)	162

Redfield Edge Primary School, Bristol

William English (9)	163
Penelope Henderson (9)	164
Poppie Palmer (8)	165
Ede Turczi Blair (10)	166
James Dheilly (9)	167
Rowan Haddrell (9)	168
Ava Woodham (9)	169
Jakob Fudge (9)	170
Ethan Clift (9)	171
Sonny Graham (9)	172
Scarlett Saunders-Rawlings (9)	173
Nevaeh Newland (9)	174
Evalyn Webb (8)	175
Olivia Saunders (8)	176

Sophia Bird (9)	177
Jack Watkins (9)	178
Isaac Purvis (8)	179
Darcey Lonergan (8)	180
Fynley Burke (9)	181
Harry Haskins (8)	182
Lucas Henley (8)	183
Joshua Moate (8)	184
Toby Piotrowski (9)	185
Daniel Bullock (9)	186
Isla Anderson (9)	187
Josh Moore (9)	188

St Kevin's Primary School, Bargeddie

Laurie Elizabeth Hastings (9)	189
Phoebe Gregory (9)	190
Matthew Atley (9)	191
Oscar Kaney (9)	192

St Stephen's CE Primary School, Bury

Ishraj Arora (10)	193
Lewis (10)	194
Ali Bilal (9)	195
Rob Keegan (9)	196
Bradley Oscar Todd (10)	197
Sammi Minhas (10)	198
Minahil Iqbal Raza (10)	199
Archie Hardman (10)	200
Joshua Adegoke (9)	201
Hadi Abdul (9)	202
Holliemae Newton (10)	203
Amir Muhsin (10)	204
Hamda Irfan (10)	205
Nathanael Thorne (10)	206
Benjamin Ryan (9)	207

THE CREATIVE WRITING

Pirates Vs Dragons

Mrs Plum (a purple dragon) was doing her work,
When suddenly a crash left a slash in a building near the shore.
As she looked out her window,
She saw...
The pirates!
"Yarr! We want yerr land!" they shouted,
As Mrs Plum ran over with other dragons.
"You'll have to fight for it!" she replied,
"How about a good ol' footy match? Yarr!"
The dragons frowned, but agreed to the plan.
"Fine, but you're gonna lose!" said Draco.
They arrived at the pitch,
As dancing tables and chairs were cheering the dragons,
The fairies forced to cheer for the pirates.
The first minute was 4-0 to the pirates.
"In yarr face! You're never going to win!"
The second half, Draco scored two goals!
4-2 to the pirates!
Oh no, the pirates hand-ball! And Flame scores!
And another! Draco scores too! 5-4 to the dragons!
The fairies are free and pirates are back to sea.

Aaleyah Mahmud (11)
Ashley Academy, South Shields

The Weird Wizard Dream

In the forest of darkness, I saw light,
And in the black, it glistened so bright,
"Oh, my dear Weird Wizard," I said,
"Is this a dream? Am I lying in bed?"

He used a little stick as a wand,
And pointed it to turn the portal into a wonderful pond,
Out came a royal queen,
Out came an adventurous teen,
Out came a dinosaur,
Along with its gigantic roar,
Out came a pirate with a bundle of gold,
Out came a fairy with a story never to be told.

Suddenly, a spark came out of my hand,
While a strike of lightning struck the land,
"I have superpowers!" I said,
It may as well have been written in bold.

Then, there was ringing to my right,
But there was nobody left in sight,
Not the queen,
Not the teen,
Not the dinosaur,

And its gigantic roar.
Not the pirate with the gold,
Not the fairy with the story, never to be told,
Not the wonderful pond,
Not even the wizard with the stick wand.

My suspicions were right,
My bedroom was now in sight,
I let out a smile and said,
"I'll be back tonight, when I go back to bed."

Kate Newton (10)
Ashley Academy, South Shields

Autumnal Dream City

Tia walked beside the glistening, glass-like lake, thinking things through.
She wondered if others had dreams like this too?
The orange, autumnal leaves that once hung upon the branches of tall, bare trees, were now littered all over the ground.
They had all gracefully glided down in the air by the pound.
Tia reached a door.
She diligently opened it and crept inside, to find that she could fly.
Of course, she seized the chance to defy gravity
And started floating around the sunset orange sky.
She couldn't believe she could fly!
Unicorns majestically zoomed past her, as she went down deeper into the depths of the sky.
Strangely, she started to go down... and down... and down, until she was on the floor.
Tia hopped over to her house, which was on the other side of the street, and opened the door.
She quietly made her way to her room and tiptoed in, then lay down on her bed.
She was back just in time for bedtime.

Gracie-Mae Robb (10)
Ashley Academy, South Shields

Birds Flying Free

In the sky, I feel free,
Finding comfort in the clouds,
Creating a nest in this tree.

In my nest, I'll lie down,
Sum up all my thoughts but I can't help it, you see,
I stare at the sky pondering the crown,
Who should win it? Me, me, me.

However, no one seems to notice at all,
Like I'm not good enough for the crown.
But they don't know me nearly as well as I know me,
I'm the coolest gull around,
I can get through anything life throws at me.

I don't miss a beat,
I don't get soggy shoes, I don't use my feet!
I soar through the sky with my powerful wings,
Ignoring any unimportant things.

As long as you know you are kind and beautiful too,
As gorgeous as this gull,
Who cares that you're not noticed,
You're perfectly, beautifully you!

Delta Miller (8)
Ashley Academy, South Shields

A Girl, A Black Cat And A Place They Call Home

Where fairies fly high, high, high. Where trees glow and rainbows sparkle an amazing sight. A black cat strolls along a great waterfall falling down a great fall! A girl skips along the long cobbled path. Her dress with colours bright falls to her feet as the black cat comes closer to her. They stride along together happy as can be. They run to a tree, the tree as dark as can be. The girl picks up the cat, and soon the cat is glowing bright, bright.
"I just needed a little magic you see," says the cat as it strides away. This time, not as gloomy as once before. With every step, a tale unfolds of friendship, magic and secrets untold. In the enchanted forest, she will forever roam, since it used to be a girl, a black cat and a place she will always call home.

Hayley Airey (10)
Ashley Academy, South Shields

The Untitled Dream

Who did it? Who took the magical ruby? Who is the thief of the stolen ruby? Will it be easy or hard to find out? Who did it? Who did it? Will we find out? Was it her? We don't know. Will we fail or succeed? Will we spot the person out or not? Who will it be? Who will it be? Will we find out? Will we find evidence or not? Will there be a trace or not? Will any other things be stolen or not? Will we see anything or not? I want to find out, you want to find out, everybody wants to find out. I want to find out, I really want to, please make it very easy! Will you help us or not? I just want to find out though, please help us. We just want to know who stole the ruby. We need to find out. Come on, come on, let's find out, let's find out who did it once and for all.

Isaac Dunlop (8)
Ashley Academy, South Shields

Once Upon A Dream

Once there was a dream,
Not where you have to work as a team,
But a miraculous trial.
On your journey you may have to be mindful,
Your surroundings may be frightening,
Or you may even experience lightning,
But remember in your heart there's a spark,
This spark won't leave a mark,
It's a spark of hope,
You may think this is a nope,
This journey may be high risk,
Your walk will have to be brisk,
A journey of a lifetime starts with one footstep,
You may come across every concept,
It is hard to know where,
But it's there,
If you believe,
You may receive,
Be real,
You don't have to shout or swear,
So remember it's always somewhere.

Alicia Waite (9)
Ashley Academy, South Shields

On The Night Of The Galaxy Moon

On the night of the galaxy moon, the sky so gloom, the stars were shining brightly.
I awoke to me sitting on a purple bee,
This lovely night turned into a nightmare.
I was pushed off, this wasn't fair!
What did I do to face this doom?
As I looked to my side, where the moon was,
I was ready for my fate, late at night.
The galaxy moon turned into a blood moon.
Did I play too much Zelda?
I tried to wake up.
Just to find, this was real.
I was starving, so I tried to get a meal.
Nothing happened.
I awaited my fate, it was still late.
Is this my life now, or is this fantasy?
There was no escape from this reality.
The galaxy moon was bad luck.
I eventually gave up.

Freja Best (10)
Ashley Academy, South Shields

The Mystical Typewriter

A girl felt like she could reach the sky
On her tiptoes, yes that high
She documented this on her typewriter
Suddenly, mysterious purple smoke appeared
Everything got bigger in an instant
But bigger things got distant
A fluttering sound came from behind
Until she said, "Oh my!"
Wing waving rapidly
She was a fairy, yes indeed
As she jumped on the keys of the typewriter
Purple smoke appeared once again
She felt as strong as a lion combing its mane
As she got bigger, things got smaller
Taller she got
Her wings vanished, without any trail of a fairy
She was back to normal just in time for dinner.

Harlo-Rose Brown (11)
Ashley Academy, South Shields

The Magic Dream Came To Life

Once upon a time, there lived a girl called Rosey. Rosey was ten years old and she had amazing dreams one night. One of her special jars, her pink one, spilt and her dream came to life. She was shocked because it was a pet dragon! She was shocked, there were happy tears.
Her mam was angry because she had a dragon. Her dad laughed so hard he started to cough. The dragon breathed fire and lit a candle. The dragon knocked the TV. Her mam shouted at the dragon. The dragon got angry and breathed flaming fire at the mam.
Rosey calmed him down but he accidentally breathed fire again. Her dad was still laughing.

Dominic Burns (8)
Ashley Academy, South Shields

A King And A Queen

There was once a king and a queen.
Tall as can be.
They had looked into the sky, but didn't know why.
They saw the sweet birds flying so high.
Then decided that they wanted to fly.
So they collected feathers from all over the kingdom.
The queen demanded everyone to sing for her.
But as they started singing,
All of a sudden they both vanished into thin air,
But it turns out that they were right up there,
Up there flying so very high,
Right up in the sky.
They put on a beautiful, elegant show,
Just like the birds they had seen before.

Enya-Rose Fisher (10)
Ashley Academy, South Shields

Red Dragon

A breath of fire, wings span wide,
In my slumber, a dragon indeed,
Eye to eye, I am astonished.

Where am I? I wish I knew,
He looks magical yet scary too,
Puff puff, spitting flames of fire in every direction.

A quick thought, but can I run?
I feel stuck, stuck in this weird place,
I am alone, no one near to help.

In the blue sky, he flies high,
Hey, hey you. Uh-hum I keep steering,
He can talk! Maybe no harm but friendly.

Before I know it, Mum wakes me up,
The world of dreams, I wish I found out.

Ethan Mukuruva (10)
Ashley Academy, South Shields

Untitled

When I go to sleep,
I dream of the galaxy,
Far beneath,
The depths of the world,
Lie in my dreams,
Hope, wonder and magic,
All there for reality,
The moonlight is calming,
Relaxing with deep sea sounds,
Wonder walks slow,
Hope comes past,
Magic is a spirit,
Keeping to entertain,
People can do work,
For others to be told,
Children learn from teachers
To become what they can
Decisions depend on words,
Questions to ask,
Spread the world with joy
Fulfil what we want,
A warming poem to be told.

Kiam Salik (8)
Ashley Academy, South Shields

The Frog On The Log

There once was a frog
Who lived on a log
Who lived all on his own.

There once was a dog
Who loved the log
That the frog called home.

The dog wanted to play
The frog wanted to stay
The log lay in dismay.

The dog snatched the log
The frog tried to hog
The log from the dog
No, the dog hogged the log.

The frog sat in dismay
The frog found a log
Where no dogs
Could hog the log.

The frog lives on a log
Sill today.

Finley Errington (10)
Ashley Academy, South Shields

Rainbows Everywhere

Rainbows, rainbows, everywhere
Flying through the crystal air.
Up above the world so high
Shining diamonds in the sky.
I can see the luminous glow
Shining bright from down below.
Rainbows, rainbows, in the sky
How I wish that I could fly.
To slide down its colourful glow
And find the pot of gold below.
Rainbows, rainbows, up above
The type of weather that I love.
A magical place where unicorns play
I wish that I could be there someday.

Eva Swinbanks (9)
Ashley Academy, South Shields

Just A Dream

J ackie (my best friend) awakens me
U nique colours swirl around me
S imultaneous birds soar in the distance
T riumphant dancers leap near me.

A nd outstanding flowers bloom outside my house.

D rastically everything suddenly disappears
R ed, orange, yellow rapidly becomes grey
E ven Jackie disintegrates
A nd then strangely I wake up
M aking me know it was just a dream.

Isla Rothery (11)
Ashley Academy, South Shields

Magic Butterfly

In fields of magical dreams
Butterflies play along the streams
Leaving behind a shimmering glow
The butterflies glide towards the rainbow
In the fluffy clouds in the skies above
Twinkling and dancing with lots of love
Singing fairies with lots of joy
Spreading pixie dust around the boy
He stops and stares into the sky
As he watches the butterflies and waves goodbye
In a world so bright and blue
A magical journey just for you.

Aliza Wilson (7)
Ashley Academy, South Shields

A World Of Craze!

The day I was getting paid for my job, I also adopted a dog.
I brought him home, so he wasn't alone,
I gave him a treat, but he did not eat,
Instead, he took my seat!
I told him off, and he flew up into the sky,
I don't know why, he didn't even say goodbye!
I went to bed, just like Mum said,
And cuddled Ted.
I don't know if the dog will come back,
Maybe he's the one on your lap!

Jasmine Hobbs (8)
Ashley Academy, South Shields

Just Dream

Up in the sky,
It's a perfect place to fly,
Even more so with a dragon,
Way better than riding a wagon,
High in the fluffy clouds,
It's not at all loud,
But then I begin to shake,
And then realise I am awake,
But I will not give up,
For I will dream of a pup,
If I shake,
And become awake,
I shall go back to sleep,
And climb a mountain so steep.

Zoe Harvey (9)
Ashley Academy, South Shields

My Cat Stole My Hat

I went to the park with my cat called Clarke.
I was wearing my hat until the cat stole my sun hat.
The hat, my lucky cat hat, was stolen by my cat.
The cat stole my hat. Get that cat!
My cat stole my hat. Get that cat!
If you don't get my hat my cat will choke.
Get that cat! My cat stole my hat.
My lucky cat, not my cat, stole my hat. Get that cat!

Matilda Envy (8)
Ashley Academy, South Shields

Dream Big Dreams

I dream big dreams about the moon,
I dream big dreams about dolphins,
I dream big dreams about dolphins jumping over the moon,
I dream big dreams about the deep sea,
I dream big dreams about the sun,
I dream big dreams about my future,
I dream big dreams about my friends,
I dream big dreams about my family,
I dream big dreams about me.

Peyton Elliott (8)
Ashley Academy, South Shields

Magical

M ost wonderful things I've ever seen
A mazing fairies flying between
G olden unicorns prancing about
I 'd never ever had a doubt
C ars zooming above as they fly
A stronauts having lots of fun in the sky
L ittle aliens in their rockets holding on to mechanical parts in their pockets.

Bobbi Price (10)
Ashley Academy, South Shields

A Painter's Canvas

Anything could be a painter's canvas,
Rocks, stones,
Eggs and bones,
The vast majority of things in the world,
Can have a painting on them,
Walls, floors,
Tables and doors!
With strokes of brushes,
Anything can be painted on,
A canvas is anything,
A canvas can go from A to Z,
Oh, what a canvas can be.

Isla Forrester (9)
Ashley Academy, South Shields

The Nightmare

In a dream so sweet and fair,
A girl danced on clouds with flair,
But as she twirled in the sky so high,
Her joy turned to fear as she started to fly.

Through the fluffy clouds, she fell,
Her dream transformed into a spell,
The once lovely scene now a frightful sight,
Yet she woke up safe, bathed in a gentle light.

Eden Lodge (11)
Ashley Academy, South Shields

Losing A Tooth

Waiting and waiting,
Pulling and pulling,
Chomping and chomping,
Checking and checking.
Just to find out my tooth is still there!
So I wait, wait, wait, chew, chew, chew, check, check, check, pull, pull, pull.
Then I chomp, chomp, chomp into an apple and my tooth falls out.
I am so happy, I sing as if I am in a chapel!

Savannah Ruane (10)
Ashley Academy, South Shields

Fairies Magical

Magical fairies play in the sun,
They have so much fun.
They fly high in the sky,
Like a bird in the sky.
They play all day, making magic like magicians,
Because they have competitions.
With this magic, the magician fairies are fun,
Especially when they are good.
Remember, fairies for life!

Bella (8)
Ashley Academy, South Shields

The Girl Who Loved Everything

Once upon a time, there was a girl called Bella.
She loved Nutella.
She loved to play in the park in the dark
And in the park she loved to play darts
And she loved to draw math charts.
Bella liked hearts and cars
And her favourite planet was Mars.

Skyler Fisher (8)
Ashley Academy, South Shields

Unicorns Flying High

When I lie in bed, late at night,
I dream that unicorns fly out of my sight.
While the winds are blowing high,
The stars sparkle in the night sky.
But, one day, the moon doesn't come,
The unicorns gossip, like, "What's wrong?"

Isabel Bates (9)
Ashley Academy, South Shields

All A Fantasy Needs

Oh, to live to love,
Witness the sky above,
To love life you must care,
Don't be bothered to share,
Oh, to be chosen,
You must be unspoken,
To have the fantasy you need,
You need to have joy and plead.

Dylan Yeeles (9)
Ashley Academy, South Shields

Thought Bubbles Of Fire

I dream. I dream as hot as the sun
As far as my dreams go
They will always flame in pride of fire
Fire and flames are all the same
Flames and flames are in my brain.

Theo Walker (7)
Ashley Academy, South Shields

Fortnite

In my room playing Fortnite.
My best friend Tom by my side.
Jumping out of the battle bus.
Gliding to Reckless Railways.
A shield needed! Tom and I are 100 100.
We find the orbs that suck us into the game.

Me and Tom are so scared, we jump up and down in fear.
There's an MPC and he says if we die it's game over.
But we can hire him, if we think we win without him.
So let's hire him. We travel to Mount Olympus.
And defeat Zeus.

We find two Duos fighting each other.
Before we know it, there are twenty-four people.
Left. We finished that now.
Having twenty people.
They have crowns, so if we win we will get a crown win.
Twenty seconds later there's one Duo left.
On Floating Island we battle.
And win so we get the crown win.

Evan Kempe (10)
Chagford CE Primary School, Chagford

My Socks Are Lost!

It was on a Monday morning,
Before the start of school,
I was sitting up in bed,
And staring at the wall,
Mum's voice floated in and said,
"You're still lazing around up there!
I need you down here! Come, get a move on,
Before I come up there!
"You need some nice new socks,
They're down here in the washing box."
But when I looked, they were all odd,
"Oh no," I moaned. "You silly sock,"
So I went to school, with, alas, my sister's pair,
But wherever I went,
There was someone to stare.

Frida Lawrence (11)
Chagford CE Primary School, Chagford

My Dream For The Future

When I am in bed,
Things go through my head,
When people are playing,
I am praying.

But before,
My life wasn't hardcore,
I used to be a child,
And now I'm wild,
My dreams for the future,
I need to have a sense of humour.

If I'm going to stress,
I might as well rest,
When it's time,
I might whine.

When I am proud,
There is always a crowd,
People always think I'm fine,
But it's like I'm living a life of crime.

If you want to know who I am,
A little fact, I have many exams,
And I'm Grace,

And I can't even tie a lace,
And people say I'm smart,
And others say I don't have a heart.

And in school,
People treat me like a fool,
And I still come,
When we can't even chew gum,
If I want to be a doctor,
Then I have to get smarter,
If I want to be a hero,
I have to stop being a weirdo.

To save the population,
I have to do an operation,
To get good reviews,
I have to be on the news,
To put my enemies to shame,
I need to have fame.

If I want to make my parents proud,
Then I have to stand my ground,
If I want to make progress,
I have to work harder than everyone else,
Before, I wasn't the best,
And I wasn't always this stressed.

All of my haters,
Are probably going to work as waiters,
Without a doubt,
I can do no working out.

Half of the media,
Have never used an encyclopedia,
I need to have stress,
To have success.

Grace Adebogun (9)
Grace Mary Primary School, Oldbury

A Trip Down Memory Lane

M emories, when I close my eyes and sometimes drool I feel like I'm going back to the school.
E veryone is scared but not me because I'm prepared, as I walk down the lane I trip and scream in pain.
M y second day of nursery, things begin to get real as I scream, "Yay" during a lesson I pinch my shin.
O h, as the bell rang for lunchtime I ran outside and the sun began to shine.
R osie red cheeks are what I have so I ran home and saw my Auntie Charlie, she calls me Rosie Posie, it always puts a smile on my face, I've found my place.
I looked up in awe, I saw a dinosaur but luckily I was in the cinema, I was amazed as I ate my cinnamon roll.
E very duck I saw I wanted to see more, only as I was in awe I nearly outsmarted my mother, another duck went in my pocket, I ran as fast as a rocket.
S ometimes I hit my head but this time was different, I hit my head on the bath, next minute I was in hospital. I only had a scar, it was shaped like a star, it was bizarre.

Alicia Westwood (9)
Grace Mary Primary School, Oldbury

The Dream Of Neverland

I just close my eyes for a little nap, not knowing ahead about this wonderful story I read.
Mother told us to get some water from the river.
It was extremely cold so it gave us a shiver.
We saw something odd, it gave me a shock.
I couldn't believe what was behind that rock.
A bright light shining out,
Behind it, I heard a deep shout.
"Come here, girls," is what it said.
Some did and I couldn't believe what we saw.
I wanted to stay.
I saw Peter Pan, he was in a battle with Captain Hook.
I wanted Peter Pan to win so I crossed my fingers for luck.
They were battling for life.
Hook even had a sharp pocket knife.
It was getting tense but Peter Pan took the win.
I couldn't help but show my grin.
In Neverland there was a beautiful blue sky.
Would you believe it if I told you I could fly?

The rainbows were colourful, they nearly blinded my eyes.
Peter Pan called me, it was a total surprise.

"Come fly with me, amongst the shooting stars."
We went that high I thought we were in Mars.
I wish I could stay in Neverland forever.
But we say goodbye and promise we'll be back.
And say, "Never say never!"

Willow Cains (8)
Grace Mary Primary School, Oldbury

A Dream Of Growing Up Again

As I close my eyes,
My energy dies,
When I fall asleep, you won't wake me,
My sleep is too deep,
But when I dream, when I imagine,
I imagine growing up again - with you by my side,
I dream that I was a tiny tot,
Drinking pretend cups of tea out of my polka dot pot,
We went on so many holidays, we had so much fun,
I wish I was back in Spain - though sometimes it wasn't sunny,
As a little girl, there was nothing to stress about,
I just sang my heart out though sometimes I did shout,
Playing with my friends and family is what I love to do,
My first day of school was amazing - everything was so new,
With friends to play with everything is great,
Other than staying up late,
When growing up you miss your childhood,
I miss all the polka dots but life is still good,
I'm chilling with friends looking at beautiful gems,

It's year two and on my way to Paris,
It's time to say my goodbyes,
We're in Paris, love is in the air,
Let's go look at the Eiffel Tower, I heard it's rare,
In the only hotel, movie night's on,
We fall asleep, we're gone.

Kellie Brittain (9)
Grace Mary Primary School, Oldbury

Hallways Of Memories

As I close my eyes, there are millions of doors,
Each filled with a memory, what are yours?
The first door I opened was when I was born,
Would you believe it was the crack of dawn?
The second door was when I got my hamster,
Called Chungus, fur like silk, he truly loves us.
The third door came with a bit of a fright,
I cracked my dad's phone - we nearly had a fight.
The fourth door was when I hurt my head,
For three weeks I was stuck in a hospital bed.
The fifth door's handle took me to the clearest shore,
Binoculars ready, I'm eager to explore.
The sixth door was in Hell,
It wasn't good, I could tell.
I opened the seventh door,
I went back in time, I heard a dinosaur roar.
The eighth door was the best one yet,
I went skydiving! I had no regret.
This was the ninth one, a monster was chasing me,
I was forced to run.
The last door was here until I had to go back,
I was given £1,000 in a rucksack!

There are so many doors to go through,
Each filled with something new!

Carter Babington (9)
Grace Mary Primary School, Oldbury

The Haunted TV

I wake up in my dreams,
But it's not what it seems.

I'm in a room,
But it was my doom.

The TV had a glitch,
The room turned dark pitch.

Grace went to touch it, tap, tap, tap,
Before you know, zap, zap, zap.

She's in a world with no charisma,
Or even sigma.

This is where we face our biggest fear,
Would you like to go here?

Carter had an attempt to save Grace A,
But he had to pay.

A room of knives,
Sits with scythes.

Ismail tried to fix it,
But he accidentally pricked it.

He was a hider,
From a giant spider.

Elrad touched it just to play,
But he would not see another day.

A room filled with girls,
His stomach twirls.

He looks at his reflection,
His fear is rejection.

Here comes Evelyna, I pushed her in,
An attempt to win.

She's in the dark and she is alone,
With a world that is unknown.

Ezra Agbebi (9)
Grace Mary Primary School, Oldbury

A Dream About My Crazy Class

When I went to bed,
Crazy thoughts about my class ran through my head,

All the children were weird and different,
There was Alicia, who dangled like a bat,
And Carter smelt like a rat,
Kellie even had a hairy ginger cat.

The girls all had worms in their hair,
The boys brought lots of germs in the air.
There was Ezra, who was always groaning and moaning,
And I don't know who Elrad was phoning.

The strangest thing was that
The head teacher travelled around on a flying mat,
She looked like a wicked witch,
And her breath smelt like a rotten sandwich.

I can't forget Esther, who slithered like a snake,
And there was Piper, who ate Evelyn's cornflakes,
Penny went to school on her toy train,
Olivia even had a mechanical brain.

Ismail, who came up from the dead,
Grace S who ate her head and the shed.
It might seem crazy, but it's certainly true,
Come visit my class, they'd love to see you!

Ezzmai Lunn (9)
Grace Mary Primary School, Oldbury

Intergalactic Fairy World

When I close my eyes and enter my dream,
I see myself in space with my fairy team,
There's Holly, who has telekinetic powers,
And Alice, who grows gorgeous galaxy flowers.

Together, we travel amongst the shooting stars,
We love all plants, especially Mars!
The poor aliens are always losing control of their machines,
We love to eat their galactic lollipops, it's the best cuisine.

The magical moon is our place to go,
On Tuesday on Jupiter, there's an amazing galaxy show.
Every day of adventure, it gets more and more terrible,
But there was no case that was bad enough, than the day of 29/09/29,
It was unbearable.

It was an alien that was robbed,
Oh, how she sobbed,
"We'll find it," I said worriedly,
We ran speedily.

After a while, we beat him (the robber),
"You will get your stuff back before November!" I said to the alien.

Piper Bates (9)
Grace Mary Primary School, Oldbury

My Week Of Wild Dreams

O h, I've had so many crazy dreams this week,
N ever would I say but... I had a beak!
C entipedes circled me in Tuesday's dream,
E vil little things... thought I was an ice cream!

U gh... Wednesday's dream, I flew on a wild cat,
P eppers could talk! So we had a crazy chat.
O nly I have got this sort of imagination,
N everland is a place I can go in this magic train station.

A nd many other dreams like Thursday's - octopus flowers,

D ragons were everywhere because of my cool powers.
R ed, orange, yellow, green, blue plus purple rainbows to look at,
E lephants fly with the wings of an eagle plus the wings of a bat!
A n abundance of ideas flow through my head,
M e and my dreams - I wonder what next week will bring.

Esther Parkes (9)
Grace Mary Primary School, Oldbury

The Night Of The Living Dummy

M ine was a dream when I went to sleep
Y ou won't believe what I saw
S o I saw a scary movie but I was reading a book when I fell asleep
T o my surprise, I was in a book and I leaped!
E arlier I saw an invisible man
R ight then I just hit him with a pan
I was in awe, it was a monster so I ran
O ut the window, up the stairs
U nknowingly I didn't know where
S ince then I knew I was in a dream.

K icked the monster (it was extreme)
I didn't know what I needed but I wanted to find a team
L *iar*
L *iar*
E very voice in my head said, *fire!*
R ight, I saw a living dummy! As soon as I touched it, my dream got crushed.

Elrad Agbebi (8)
Grace Mary Primary School, Oldbury

Mythical Magic

When I drifted off to sleep
I had a bit of a weep
Not of sadness
Just of happiness
I was out in my backyard
I was playing really hard
Then stairs appeared
When I climbed them clouds cleared
I saw the mythical creatures
While I tried to figure out their features
When I looked in the water
It was bright of colour
Unicorns galloped past me
There was a fairy I guarantee
Dragons breathing fire
Mermaids in a choir
Wizards making potions
Even a witch made an explosion
It looked so real
I think I had to conceal
But to my surprise when I went underwater
I saw a mermaid, she was the younger daughter

When I woke up
I poured water from a cup
It was just a dream
But I'm going to get ice cream.

Kavya Shah (8)
Grace Mary Primary School, Oldbury

My Memory Doors

I woke up in a strange dream,
Things were not as they seem.

There's more than a hundred doors,
And there's probably even more floors.

I opened the first door at last,
And I was shocked to see memories from the past.

The first door I opened was when I slept at my BFF's house,
The dream was vivid, next to me was a doll's house.

I was at the second door,
Which was on the first floor.

In this, I was in the sky,
Riding on a roller coaster, really high.

Drayton Manor is a place I really love,
Feeling free like the birds above.

The third door was when I was really small,
I grazed my knee, it was a nasty fall.

I can't wait to sleep to see which memories are next!

Evelyna Welsh (8)
Grace Mary Primary School, Oldbury

The Haunted House

When I closed my eyes, it gave me a fright. I entered a haunted house, and the lonely piano played a strange tune. I looked behind me, there was an evil man. He locked the doors except for one at the back.
Evie and Angel were with me, ready to attack. We scanned the room looking to hide. There was a door to the basement at the side. We hurried down the stairs, he chased us. We had no choice other than to move swiftly.
Through the window, we escaped at last. We ran down the hill extremely fast. We looked behind us, he was still there with his greasy, long, filthy hair. He was catching up with us. He was by our side. We were so scared, we almost cried.
That's when I realised it was just a dream, there was no reason for me to scream.

Alliyah Hall (9)
Grace Mary Primary School, Oldbury

A Dream For My Future

A fter I wake, I picture the stadium,
S omewhere where joy brings me,
P eace calms me down ready for game time,
I nspirational athletes training in my head, I wonder what will happen next,
R unners ready as the track eagerly waiting for the pistol to sound,
A thletes off ready to race, who will win the exhilarating race?
T he finish line approaches closer and closer, our hearts are beating,
I was first and fleeing to the finish line,
O n the track, the finish line was in front of me,
N early the end for the other athletes, but it was I who won! I hope your future, like mine, is happy and bright.

Jovan Sandhu (9)
Grace Mary Primary School, Oldbury

My Dream Of The Perfect World

Last night I had a wonderful dream,
The world was different, people were working as a team.
No matter where you came from everyone got along,
The incredible sense of unity was so strong.
Everywhere I looked people wore a smile,
No one was ever hostile.
People opened doors for each other and said good morning as well,
I knew the humans living in this world loved it, I could just tell.
The trees were a beautiful emerald green, they were healthy too,
The glistening oceans streaming across the horizon were the clearest of blue.
No animals in bad condition,
And all of the children were helping and had huge ambitions.

Danyal Shah (9)
Grace Mary Primary School, Oldbury

My Volcanic Dream

When I went to sleep, I had a dream,
It was amazing until there was a lava stream.

A volcano, I had to explore,
However, I did not know what was next door.

I was shaken from left to right,
I looked up, and it gave me a fright.

Smoke was billowing into the sky,
I knew people were bound to cry.

The lava ran swiftly,
I needed to think quickly.

Through the forest as thick as can be,
Then I saw snakes coming toward me.

When I felt like I was going to die,
I woke up and realised, it was just a lie.

Grace Smith (9)
Grace Mary Primary School, Oldbury

My Biggest Fear In A Dream

The plane is descending uncontrollably with
Hope all engines will light up before hitting the
mountain range
Eager to climb out of the dive, I've got to fix this
Plummeting, I do a restart procedure
Luckily the plane's four engines restart and I've put
A lot of room between my plane and the mountain
Now cruising back to Jakarta tragedy strikes
Even the most experienced pilot could not fix this
I'm petrified all engines die, landing now seems
impossible
Satan struck and all engines are off and the plane is
Falling.

Frankie Byrne (9)
Grace Mary Primary School, Oldbury

Candy House

C an you see people walking down the gummy bear street?
A dding candy decorations on the seat
N ow opening the door to see toffee trees
D reaming all about the cotton candy clouds
Y ou can see everyone dreaming about unicorns and rainbows

H ouses are defined with candy everywhere
O cean-like chocolate river flowing with candy boats
U s dancing to be lucky
S eeing every lollipop in the world
E verywhere we go to look we see lots of candy and chocolate.

Ruby Cheshire (8)
Grace Mary Primary School, Oldbury

A Dream For My Teacher

M y dream for you Miss O, is that you're always happy and healthy
Y ou work so hard - surely you should be wealthy?

T his dream is kind and I want you to know
E ach one of us loves you and we hope your future glows
A nd I dream that you will be a teacher forever
C hildren you teach always end up so clever
H opefully, my dreams for you will come true
E verything in my life is perfect with you
R emember to rest and not be a pest.

Angel Davis (9)
Grace Mary Primary School, Oldbury

Candy House

C otton candy clouds swirling in the sky,
A nd toffee trees dancing up so high.
N ow I see gummy bears coming alive,
D reaming of the candy house falling apart,
Y earning for a world of candy sweets.

H ouses are decorated with marshmallows to eat.
O cean chocolate rivers flowing oh so grand,
U nder the candy roofs, all feels right, a magical land.
S weet memories made day and night.
E ndless sweetness in every way.

Olivia Woolley (9)
Grace Mary Primary School, Oldbury

Candy House

C otton candy clouds swirling
A nd toffee trees dancing up so high
N ow I see gummy bears coming alive
D reaming of a world of candy sweets falling apart
Y earning for a world of candy so sweet

H ouses are decorated with marshmallow to eat
O cean chocolate river floating oh so grand
U nder the candy roof, all feels right, a magical land
S weet memories made my day and night
E ndless sweetness in every way.

Evie-Mai Arnold (8)
Grace Mary Primary School, Oldbury

Untitled

C otton candy clouds swirling in the sky
A nd trees dancing up so high
N ow I see gummy bears coming alive
D reaming of candy houses falling apart
Y earning for a world of candy so sweet

H ouses are decorated with more snacks to eat
O cean the chocolate flowing oh so grand
U nder the candy roofs, all feels light
S weet memories made day and night
E ndless sweetness in every way.

Skylar-Rose Hayes (9)
Grace Mary Primary School, Oldbury

I Saw A Ghost

It was midnight,
I had a fright.

It was strange,
I started to change.

I was turning invisible,
How would this be believable?

There was a banging at the door,
But then I realised it was coming from the floor.

It was coming towards me,
But then it stopped, how could this be?

I saw a ghost!
Oh, that's just me.

I went to sleep that night,
But something didn't feel right.

Minnie Flavell (9)
Grace Mary Primary School, Oldbury

The Plummeting Plane

T he plane, in a flash, is descending straight to the ground
H oping all the engines will make a sound
E ager to escape this dreadful mess.

P lane nose tilts upwards – I'm trying not to stress
L osing all control again, the nose dips down
A nd my heart beats rapidly and I begin to frown
N o one to help me, I begin to scream
E ventually, I wake up and realise it was just a dream.

Penelope Lee Williams (9)
Grace Mary Primary School, Oldbury

WWII

In my bed, I fell asleep,
I tried to wake up, but it was just too deep.
Gunshots and grenades were thrown,
We did this to keep the king on his throne.

We tried our best, but unfortunately,
The girls were under arrest.
It was up to the boys to defeat the opposition,
However, they were in a weaker position.

Eventually, though we did win,
When I awoke I felt like a winner,
I'm hungry, what's for dinner?

Kobe Bellfield-Shearwood (9)
Grace Mary Primary School, Oldbury

Gladiators

G ladiators fight while lions protect
Y ellow gates open wide
M y my my, they are starting to fight
N o one wants to see the corpse
A tticus down, no one made a sound
S neaky snakes slither around
I saac fights not knowing he's about to get a bite
U nderneath fire ants appear
M isery is struck over the town, Isaac wins with a big frown.

Ismail Ajmal (9)
Grace Mary Primary School, Oldbury

Vampire

V ast vampire approaching death,
A ssault me if you dare,
M ind, I will control your mind,
P eace, there is peace inside you,
I nside, you don't want to hurt me,
R ight, it's just you and me,
E stimate your strength.

P eace is what peace wants,
E xcellent powers,
A ngry enemies,
R aging strength inside me,
S eeing the light rising I hide,
E scalating sun.

Pearse Sheehy (11)
Hale Preparatory School, Hale

Eras Tour

The old dog I used to have,
He came back,
Was I happy or sad?
Hiton talked!
We had a walk,
To the tour,
It looked like a ball,
We went inside,
We gazed at the stage,
Then we had a blast,
Then I was awakened by my mother standing in my room.

Ela Walshaw (11)
Hale Preparatory School, Hale

Suddenly

S ilent spirits,
U ncalm,
D ead of night,
D ark as coal,
E mbrace for life,
N o, no! He screams,
L ast breath,
Y our death happened suddenly.

Esther Eckersley (11)
Hale Preparatory School, Hale

Diamond Vacation

Going to bed excited for tomorrow,
Woken up, going down the corridor, which is hallow.
I'm going on holiday!
That is today, Monday.
I need to call my friends,
To see if they are ready.
OMG, my pen! (They are singing),
My bag is really heavy.

I'm on the plane,
With my friends.
Boom! The plane lands on the runway.
I see diamond hens!
I'm going to go shopping!
I'm going there hopping.
I'm done, I am going to the hotel,
There is a motel nearby too!
I am going to the pool.
This is so cool!
(I'm excited like a dog's wagging tail).

Idil Tunc (11)
Harris Primary Academy Chafford Hundred, Grays

Is The Moon That Far Away?

On my roof, I hear a pitter-patter,
I ask myself what is the matter?
So out of my window, my head popped out,
There was a cat wanting to maybe say, "What's up?"

Then somehow, it started to climb some invisible stairs,
Enough to make me glare,
As the cat went into the night sky,
I started to follow, not saying goodbye.

I got onto the steps, muttering speechless lines of steps,
Then the cat and I saw it, the moon!
It looked like a big, bright balloon,
Then we dropped through the sea,
The wind suddenly picked up and it was time to fly.

Kouami Zewu-Manscour (11)
Harris Primary Academy Chafford Hundred, Grays

My Dreams, My Imagination

Space is as beautiful as a rainforest,
The silence is calming,
The sight of stars,
More extraordinary, you could see them from Earth,
The sight of unknown planets filling your vision!

The heavy rainfall from below,
Drip, drip, drip,
Proving peoples' thoughts wrong,
Earth isn't flat!

Items flying through space,
Whoosh,
Never-ending flight,
Soaring through space.

The moon,
As still as a statue,
Seeing the first-ever flag placed on it,
Gently waving as it sits there.

Ayan Hussain (11)
Harris Primary Academy Chafford Hundred, Grays

Spacemares

Once upon a dream,
I was deep in space,
Comfortable in a rocket ship,
It was a very dark place.

Suddenly... *creak!*
I panicked,
I was dragged out of my rocket,
I thought this was the end.

I was approaching a black hole,
But something was off,
I could breathe perfectly,
I was sucked into the black hole.

I drifted off,
There were shooting stars,
Fading images of beautiful places,
Dreams that were rainbow and gold and red.

This was space!

Dovydas Dula (11)
Harris Primary Academy Chafford Hundred, Grays

Nightmares Or Dreams

N othing has prepared me for this haunted house I see,
I take small steps, as scared as I can be.
G ruesome things, everywhere I can see,
H ow can this happen? I really don't know.
T hud! What is that noise? I will just go with the flow.
A
M anic grin spreads on its face like
A clown.
R un! I think, now he has a frown.
E yes will glow, I don't want to see its face,
S cared I am, and I think it will come and chase!

Saanvi Bolisetty (10)
Harris Primary Academy Chafford Hundred, Grays

In Bulgaria

Bulgaria is amazing,
Fun, loud and entertaining,
Lying in the green sun,
With nothing to be done.

It is as hot as a fire,
No one here is a liar,
All the trees are dancing,
The food here is enhancing.

With many exciting adventures,
In the woods, let's venture,
In a gingerbread house,
Everything is as quiet as a mouse.

The dear, blue sea,
Here is all you can see,
Many golden doors,
All decorated floors.

This is Bulgaria!

Emily Georgieva (10)
Harris Primary Academy Chafford Hundred, Grays

A Loud Silence

I wake up in my bed as the house is dead silent. Even the footsteps of a mouse could be heard. I don't know where my parents are, however, I see a bright white beam coming from the cracks of the window curtains. I jump out of bed and peer through the cracks of the dark grey curtains and just then, my eyes lock with hollow white holes as I stare at a crowd of humanoid, shadow-like figures standing outside of my bedroom window staring into my soul. And then, I wake up from my nightmare, trembling in fear.

Lily Adedipe (11)
Harris Primary Academy Chafford Hundred, Grays

The Lonely Town

Once upon a dream,
I walk into shadows,
Everything dark,
Everything narrow.

A girl, small as a fish,
Follows me,
To a small, little ditch.

She pushes me down,
Nothing to do,
Everything gone,
Except for my blue.

The girl laughs,
No one around,
I'm lost in this lonely town.

I look around, everything is silent,
Except for footsteps that become violent,
I wake up with everything found.

Helena Rose (11)
Harris Primary Academy Chafford Hundred, Grays

The Beach

The sky was shining as bright as a diamond,
The palm trees were dancing in the wind,
A coconut fell... *Thud!*

The bubbles were going as high as a kite,
The bubbles went *pop! Pop! Pop!*
The waves went *whoosh!*
A kite was staring at the heavenly clouds.

The sun was glistening glitter,
The boy had the most joy in his life,
The plants were quivering behind the shadowy tree,
A kite got lost, like in darkness.

Timas Miknevicius (10)
Harris Primary Academy Chafford Hundred, Grays

Crystals

Curled up and warm,
Enter a world,
Filled with broken dreams.

Little flower bud,
With nobody to see it,
Open anyway.

Piece back together,
What has been lost,
A shining pearl within.

Lotus flowers,
Delicate and true,
Understand in their silence.

The crystals within us,
Clear and unclouded,
Fill up the night sky,
No broken heart could deny.

Joannabel Emma Eshun (11)
Harris Primary Academy Chafford Hundred, Grays

Starlight!

Once upon a dream,
Massive starlight beams,
Singing on a stage,
Me, in a fancy magazine,
Open up a page,
Fans going wild,
Me, fully styled.

Walking a red carpet,
Everything looking starlit,
People taking pictures, *click, click*,
And my designer making stitches,
Meeting my idol,
Still rocking in style,
Remember to smile!

Sophie Chapman (11)
Harris Primary Academy Chafford Hundred, Grays

The Pirate Parade

There I was,
On an abandoned island,
Stranded.
No food,
Nothing.
Just sad, no life on this island,
And six palm trees.
As I was gazing at the bright, steaming sun,
Then I saw it,
The pirate parade ship.
I was so gullible,
I ran straight up to it with excitement,
Eyes glistening,
Mouth open,
Bigger than a wide abyss.

Edwin Kokogho (10)
Harris Primary Academy Chafford Hundred, Grays

North Moon

Deep in the forest,
By the light of the full moon,
We all turn into werewolves,
Careful, not too soon.

The pack is amazing,
We are all super strong,
But I am the alpha,
Dare you to prove me wrong.

The light shines above us,
Purple, green and blue,
They are shining from the north,
I guess you can see them too.

A magic fire roars,
The fairies hide as we howl,
But the unicorns run around us,
So we really can't be that foul.

Next time it's a full moon,
Come down to the enchanted wood,
We would like you to join our pack,
We would love it if you could.

Melody Nicholls (8)
Holsworthy CE Primary School, Holsworthy

The Vampire Diaries

I lie in my bed, a book on my head.
Then I hear a loud knock and the book begins to rock.
The knock gets louder, I open the door.
Who do I see? Jack on the floor.
How did he get there? I want to know more.
I get a nervous feeling as I go to explore.
I bump into Clara and together we go up to the attic to search for a clue.
Will we find one or will we find two?
We open the door and guess what we saw?
Alfie the Vampire flying through the door.
He bites my neck and sucks my blood.
I fly through the air and he spins me around.
I'm a vampire now, as sad as could be.
I'll never be able to roam around free.

Elsie Jourdain (10)
Holsworthy CE Primary School, Holsworthy

Royal High Beach

R ight in the middle of spring
O n the beach was a pair of friends.
Y uri and Shopnie were their names
A nd they went to the new beach in town.
L ater in the evening, their teacher joined for tea.

H appily they skipped home after.
I n the night they went to sleep before
G oing to school.
H orrifically swimming was cancelled.

B ecause of a shortage of teachers.
E very time this happened.
A nd they went back to the
C hurch for singing. They lived
H appily ever after.

Holly-Ann Neale (9)
Holsworthy CE Primary School, Holsworthy

A Famous Dancer

Once upon a time, there was a famous dancer and she always won dancing competitions. She won the dancing trophy and she adored it.
One day she noticed it was gone. Then the next day she asked all her dancing friends and they said they did not go to her friend's house. But she did not know someone was lying so she asked Kira if she could go round to Kira's house after practice and she said, "Yes, of course you can!"
When she went she saw the trophy and she told the teacher. She scolded her from practice and she got her trophy back. She kept on winning till she was too old!

Isabelle Atkins (9)
Holsworthy CE Primary School, Holsworthy

The Old Magic Key

A pair of dogs went on an adventure one day,
D ora and Amber were the names, I say.
V igorous and strong, they had to be,
E mbarking on an adventure to find the lost old magic key.
N avigating their way through the dark, damp woods,
T wisting and turning, looking for the goods.
U pstream and downstream until there, it sat,
R usty and well-used, within a smart hat.
E veryone cheered when Dora and Amber returned that day,
S afely returning the lost old magic key.

Chloe Stacey (9)
Holsworthy CE Primary School, Holsworthy

Not Tonight!

As I enter the haunted house,
I tiptoe quietly, like a mouse.
Sophie, my friend, is by my side,
We see an ogre... we run and hide.

We look downstairs and who should we see?
Auntie Lucy mixing with glee.
A great big cake, just for me!

I hear footsteps behind me,
A hand reaches out and gone is my friend Sophie.
Gone without a doubt!
Her head has been eaten.
But I have not been beaten.

I hide in a cupboard.
I shiver with fright.
Will he find me?
Not tonight!

Hannah Cholwill (10)
Holsworthy CE Primary School, Holsworthy

Dreams

I go to sleep, I close my eyes,
Knowing tomorrow will be just fine.
I wake up somewhere bright and fun,
Fairies and unicorns dancing and prancing in the cool, summer sun.
They tell me their problems that scare them all day,
Worries and issues that won't go away.
Because of a wicked woman, mean and scary,
If you see her, you must be wary.
Her name is the Wicked One,
And she used to be a nun.
I wake up from the magical night, a bright light shining on me,
I find out it was just a dream.

Erin Murdock (8)
Holsworthy CE Primary School, Holsworthy

Skittles The Dog

Hark, hark, I hear a dog bark,
I see him coming towards me,
His fur is brown, his eyes are big,
With his tongue hanging out,
I don't know if I should scream or shout.

But something tells me he's not to be feared,
This big hairy dog is friendly you see,
And I love him and he loves me.

His name is Skittles and he is my pet,
We're always together except,
When he's at the vet.

Thomas Hurst (7)
Holsworthy CE Primary School, Holsworthy

Trousers Down

Packing up our maths books,
Now it's time for PE.
I'm taking off my trousers,
And all my friends are looking at me.
My pants fall down around my feet,
And all the kids are laughing.
Even my teacher finds it funny,
Because she can see my little tummy.
I start to stir, I start to wake,
My mum is giving me a great big shake.
"Ellie Plumb,
Why can I see your bum?"

Ellie Plumb (7)
Holsworthy CE Primary School, Holsworthy

Land Of Adventure

When I go to sleep
I visit a magical world called
Land of Adventure
This place has many magical things
From dancing fairies
To alicorns, that can fly higher
Than you can see from land
Sometimes I ride on the alicorns
Sometimes I dance with the fairies
Every time I go back to the world
I wonder if it'll be gone
But it never is.

Isabella Loach (8)
Holsworthy CE Primary School, Holsworthy

Sunny Spain

Holidaying in Spain
My life will never be the same

I'm on a lilo in the pool
My dad is looking like a fool
He wears sunglasses and a hat
He jumps around like a cat

The sun is shining nice and hot
I never want to change the spot
I'm as happy as I'll ever be
And I can even see the sea.

Leyla Prouse (9)
Holsworthy CE Primary School, Holsworthy

Missing

M issing is scary
  I ncreasing my anxiety
  S trangers all around me
  S omewhere not familiar
  I have been found
  N ever doing that again
  G lancing left and right, I am home...

My mum awakens me for school
Luckily I was not lost, I was in a dream.

Beth Hammond (9)
Holsworthy CE Primary School, Holsworthy

Wicked

Witches are evil, witches are mean
If you see one you may scream
Fairies are nice, fairies can fly
If you don't believe, they may cry
Pirates are selfish, pirates are cruel
Don't be mistaken or be a fool.
Mermaids are magical, mermaids can sing
If you hear them you may have a tingle.

Amelia Matthews (8)
Holsworthy CE Primary School, Holsworthy

Dream Big Dream

Fairies are lovely, fairies are nice
If you see them you are in the dream
Witches are cruel, witches are evil
If you don't believe they will turn you into a frog
Mermaids are magical, mermaids are beautiful
If you hear them you will feel a tingle in your body.

Darina Tyschenko (8)
Holsworthy CE Primary School, Holsworthy

Ruby And Freya

Ruby and Freya
Ruby is a dog and Freya is a girl
She loves playing in the park with her dog
Then Ivy-Leigh turns up
She is Freya's sister
She is a baby
They have so much fun in the park!

Willow Read (9)
Holsworthy CE Primary School, Holsworthy

Untitled

Once upon a dream, in Year Five's gleam,
Where fantasies sparkled in a young mind's stream,
Imagination soared on wings untamed,
In a realm of possibility, dreams full of flame.

Through corridors of books and whispers of tales,
Where castles grew tall and ships set sail,
In fields of wonder where fairies danced,
And heroes rose, their destinies advanced.

In every heart, a story to tell,
Of dragons conquered and wishes to swell,
With each page turned, a world anew,
Once upon a dream, Year Five's debut.

So let the ink flow and let dreams arise,
In the playground of minds where magic lies,
For, in every child's dream, a story is born,
Once upon a dream, in Year Five's morn.

Sochi Agulanna (9)
James Wolfe Primary School Upper Campus, London

Dreams Unbound

Once upon a dream,
Where fantasies unfurl,
In the realm of imagination,
Where dreams swirl,
Where stars wink and moonbeams gleam,
In the night's embrace where reality seems.

Whispers of enchantment fill the air,
As dreams take flight without a care,
In this world where wishes gleam,
Once upon a dream where hopes redeem.

Let your pen dance on the page,
Crafting tales of joy and sage,
In this competition let your dreams gleam,
For in the land of dreams, you reign supreme.

Zella Mohammed Ziad (10)
James Wolfe Primary School Upper Campus, London

In Winter

In the quiet stillness of the winter frosty night,
The world is hushed beneath a blanket of white.
Silent flakes of snow dance around in the freezing cold air,
Creating an art piece beyond compare.
The trees stand tall, their branches bare,
The earth sleeps beneath the frosty cover,
Dreaming of the warmth it will soon discover.
Leaving a trail of icy crystals in its hand.
The world is transformed into a winter wonderland.
A magical place where dreams expand.

Rachael Skipper (10)
James Wolfe Primary School Upper Campus, London

Once Upon A Dream

Once upon a dream,
Where delicate, daring fairies roam,
Rainbows follow the pathway home.
High in the leaves, puffs of white magic float,
Cascading rivers advance the ominous boat.
Gnomes of hope stride across the vast arch,
Mini toy soldiers come alive, march, march.
Drummers form a large band,
Trumpets blow across the land.
Suddenly, I wake up in my room,
The gloomy room, lit by the moon.
Maybe, another day,
Where in the same place, I lay.

Salimatu Bibah (10)
James Wolfe Primary School Upper Campus, London

The Universe

Stars shine bright,
Glistens across the sky,
Planets rotate.
Wish upon a star tonight,
And if it's right,
Your luck will come through.

The moon, the sun,
All connected like family,
With minds, curiosity and imagination.
Stars can be made and discovered,
Where will the universe take you today?

Zoe Liscovsky Colussi (10)
James Wolfe Primary School Upper Campus, London

Dark Eerie Nights

I close my eyes every night
So the creatures don't bite
Fate is no other than fear
As people gather around and cheer

I disappear into the sky
Children filled with lies
Ominous screams fill the room
The people find their tomb.

Ella Dhue (9)
James Wolfe Primary School Upper Campus, London

Starlight

As the sky darkens every night,
There's one star that shines, brighter than a light.
Although it's far and wide,
It's still the diamond in the sky.
Nobody can see the diamond in the sky,
Because it's covered with the night sky.

Olivia Ng (9)
James Wolfe Primary School Upper Campus, London

The Sea Serpent

In my nightmares,
I found a portal,
I knew it had to be magical,
And what did I find?
Some crazy pirates trying to hide,
As the storm whipped the waves,
A monster came out of a cave,
It was a grotesque sea serpent,
Who really needed some peppermint,
Lots of pirates got hurt,
One even tried to throw dirt.
The sea serpent bit the ship,
And got hit by a giant whip,
I found bravery rushed through my body,
And pirates stopped being crazy,
They all were inspired to fight,
The sea serpent responded with an almighty bite.
I jumped and swung a sword high,
And poof! I vanished from the sky,
I was safe from my impending doom,
Then, I realised I was back in my room.

Luke Ray (9)
Manorfield CE Primary School, Stoney Stanton

Dragons Of The Blue

I'm in a cave that you will choose,
I can see a diamond,
Blue and bright as you.
As I look, I can see a dragon too.
It looks straight at me,
Then I feel happy as the Dragon of the Blue smiled,
The Dragon of the Blue is blue and kind.
Next week, I do a potion,
As it's blue, I taste it,
It makes me a magical wizard,
Even more magical.
It feels tingly, but magical,
The next day,
I left the Dragon of the Blue,
I saw another Dragon of the Blue,
It was white too,
The dragon seemed like a queen,
In the cave full of mist,
When it came to day,
It was even more magical.
Then, my Dragon of the Blue,
Is gone, gone forever,
Who knows what happened?

Mollie Clarke (9)
Manorfield CE Primary School, Stoney Stanton

The Golden Glove

In a far land,
Miles away,
There lives a beautiful Allay.
It has pixie wings,
And hangy hair,
Trying to make this land fair.
Singing songs,
And having fun,
With scary, sacred dragons.
With lethal teeth,
They fly in the sky,
Way, way up high.
This little Allay told a lie,
So she lost her wings and couldn't fly.
Losing her chances for the golden glove,
She spread her love,
And shared her toys.
But little Allay,
Got no glove.
Later that night,
Through the sea,
Was a beautiful, vivid light.
It gave Allay a fright.

There it was,
The golden glove,
Forever on her hand.
From this day,
It's her land!

Isabelle Fowkes (9)
Manorfield CE Primary School, Stoney Stanton

The Bad Dragon

Yesterday, I went to bed and I woke up at school. It was a bit weird because I heard a bang in the distance. I exploded. I saw my mum and I was happy because I was scared.

We went into a classroom and I saw a dragon. He was burning buildings down. In a blink, half of the school was on fire. Me and my mum were flabbergasted and we looked on in shock. I was petrified because it was like a 100-foot dragon.

We hid but it saw us and kidnapped us both, so we were screaming in fear. He took me and my mum into a cave and chained us up. I forgot I had bolt cutters so I did my mum's first and then she did mine. We were free. Well, that's what I thought.

We got back to the small village and I woke up...

Freddie Hayward (9)
Manorfield CE Primary School, Stoney Stanton

The Mythical Story

M onster's dark, big, humongous, green, big, red eyes
Y ucky feeling from the ceiling, fairies flying
T he big red clown chasing after me
H e was big and red, humongous
I t was so, so scary, "Hiya," I said
C all static so the call was fake
A ll around me, stalls standing
L ost from home, so scared.

S o lost, "Where am I? It is so cold here"
T he sound of raving was making me queasy
O r was it my belly? I didn't bring anything to eat
"R oar!" said the clown, so scary
"Y es," said the clown, "it's me, wake up!"

Oscar Roach (8)
Manorfield CE Primary School, Stoney Stanton

My Favourite Dream Ever!

I fall asleep and wake up in a dream land.
I can smell sweet lavender and cinnamon. Sweet, lovely food.
I see dancers, dance teachers, potions, cardboard Chichén Itzá, cardboard dinosaurs and a fun, pink and baby blue bouncy castle.
There are loads of beautiful animals, like baby bunnies, baby dogs and baby cats.
They are eating caviar with royalty.
They sleep like stealthy tigers and lethal snakes.
I get a big hug from all of them.
(In my dream of course.)
I love them all, but then I see something that makes me thrilled.
I see... my favourite... singer!
I am *so* excited. I run up to Billie Eilish...
But it is cardboard. I am fuming.

Lexi-Rae Joyce (9)
Manorfield CE Primary School, Stoney Stanton

The Magical Bookshelf

Once, there was a bright bookshelf. A little girl went into the bookshelf. It closed slowly as she walked in. *Crreeeak*, the door slowly closed. As she walked all the way in she heard a noise. It was a deer. It quickly ran through the snow. She heard her feet go through the snow.

She found a hut, then she looked back. The bookshelf wasn't there. She saw a tiny person, it was a fairy, but then she went into the hut. There was a note saying 'Dear little girl. Don't worry, this is a dream. Go back to where the bookshelf was and the bookshelf will open. Then, if you lie down on your bed, under the quilt and close your eyes and open them, you will wake up.'

Theodore Needham (9)
Manorfield CE Primary School, Stoney Stanton

The Dragon Of The Blue

Red and blue,
The dragons flew,
Indeed a man who had a lethal plan,
To kill the Dragon of The Blue,
He got parties of armies,
And he said,
"Destiny...
Destiny is a gift,
Some go their entire lives,
Living an existence of quiet desperation,
So when we go to the den of the dragon,
Don't let him push down on your shoulders,
Kill him!"
As they journeyed on their horses,
As they scurried in the long, weakening grass,
They saw the Dragon of The Blue,
As they took swings,
He swung,
And killed the dragon,
The dragon had a baby,
And killed everything in sight.

Grayson Greenland (9)
Manorfield CE Primary School, Stoney Stanton

The Zoo

It is a cool day and everything is so amazing
All the things are sparkling
It is so very, very amazing in the cool, amazing house
And the nature is so amazing
Ah! A dinosaur, but there is not just one
There are also more of them
And there is a flying dinosaur
And the zoo looks amazing
There are some tigers and lions like that
Aha! There are some elephants
And there are some hippos and rhinos just like that
And there are some monkeys, frogs
Ostriches and bears just like that
Also, a zoo keeper
Telling me to feed the zoo animals
And now I'm in the shop
And you can buy food in there.

Nicolas Regena (9)
Manorfield CE Primary School, Stoney Stanton

A Dragon In Time For Tea

Dragon, dragon, flying high,
Up, up in the sky,
Soar up high,
Dive down low,
Where will you next go?
Over the trees,
Through the lake,
You're all wet now,
Shake! Shake! Shake!
Oh no! Soggy, soggy, you've made it all boggy,
How will Miss Moggy get across now?

Dragon, dragon, flying high,
Running, hiding from human eye,
Past the trees,
Past the lake,
Running, hurrying, you'll be late,
Tick tock, tick-tock, goes the clock,
Dinner is served, it's 8 o'clock.
Back for supper,
Back for tea.
Everybody's there now. Yippee! Yippee!

Millie Fry (9)
Manorfield CE Primary School, Stoney Stanton

Mystic Magical Monster

In a land far away, these magical monsters,
Very magical monsters indeed,
Flying monsters, walking monsters, swimming monsters,
Good and evil, I don't know,
Which are which,
You can't tell.
From the sky, you can't tell at all,
I hit the ground with a thump,
The monsters heard,
I talked in their language,
They said, "Intkigbtg, latditcan."
I had no idea what they were,
Or what they said,
I ran to a hedge and hid,
But there was a monster,
Before I screamed,
He said he was good,
So I thought I was fine,
But then I woke up,
And it was all a dream!

AJ Taylor (9)
Manorfield CE Primary School, Stoney Stanton

The Wizard

One day there was a wizard,
He had magic,
But because his magic can lead to a tragic end,
Crash, bang,
Woosh,
The wizard wouldn't control his magic,
He can just make it tragic,
But one day he found a broom,
He flew up, up and away,
Bang! He landed in a tree,
He found this substance called hallucinogen,
Next thing you know,
Thud, it's on the floor,
Thud with the mud, he had mud on him,
We found a wand that was wrong,
He waved it around and around,
He died but then arrived,
Now nobody knows what or where he is.

Oliver Grant (9)
Manorfield CE Primary School, Stoney Stanton

A Nightmare To Dream

As I fell asleep on this dark night,
I suddenly woke up in a strange twilight,
Blazing clouds at such a height,
This wasn't my real world,
What a fright!

Towering buildings built to loom,
All I could feel was a sense of doom,
Shaking lights went past with a zoom,
I felt like I was trapped in a dreaded room.

Not where I belong, feeling helpless,
Feeling weird and all alone,
My heart was filled to the brim with sadness,
Oh, how I wish I was safe at home.

I saw your people in the distance until
I wondered what next evil will they kill?

Eliza Bennett (9)
Manorfield CE Primary School, Stoney Stanton

Royal Dragon

R oyal dragon in my dreams, every night in his,
O wn castle,
Y ou and me, we go on mighty adventures every night,
A ll we do is explore your desolate world,
L ord, my majestic, towering dragon, rise and take me to your castle.

D ragon, this huge, mighty castle is bigger than you,
"**R** oar!" shouts the dragon,
"**A** hh!" I scream, calm down,
"**G** o!" says the dragon. "It is nearly daytime."
"**O** h yes, bye."
N ow that was so good, I hope it happens next time.

Milen Rowe (8)
Manorfield CE Primary School, Stoney Stanton

Mythical Creatures!

M agical creatures all around, staring into a blank space not found
Y ou need to hide, some are coming in the sky, and stars are bright
T hey're here all around, blinded by the sky, falling to the ground
H ey, finally they're gone, no need to worry, they're far gone
I t's getting dark, run there, here again, ready to hunt
C almly she ran far away into the forest and was not scared one bit
A ll along she was young, not scared far gone!
L ater that night stars shone bright, and finally she appeared with not one tear.

Honey Seaton (9)
Manorfield CE Primary School, Stoney Stanton

Dragons Land

Once upon a time, the red, the blue and the yellow dragons flew.
While the monsters grew, the wizards cast midnight spells, with all the crazy, funky smells. Finally the dragons land came at peace.
Until the purple dragon came! As soon as it landed, the day went to night. It seemed that the king of the land - or should I say the mighty wizard - had a fight.
When the day came people cheered but everyone knew that the wise man with the beard would win if the kings of the underworld came to help the purples. So sadly, the wizard had to let the dragons land down. So what would happen to the dragons?

Seth Currie (9)
Manorfield CE Primary School, Stoney Stanton

Jurassic Park

J ust as I walk out of the elevator
U nder my shoes, I see a footstep of a dinosaur
R earing through the bushy greenery. Run!
A dinosaur comes and roars as loud as a fierce lion
S ee it fly above my head
S neakily
I walk around a cave and see...
C ave people!

P anicky, we run away from the dinosaur
A T-rex grabs us and drools over our heads
R aging raptors chase us, chew us and step on us
K indly they let us go and I walk back to the elevator.

Olly Brewin (8)
Manorfield CE Primary School, Stoney Stanton

Space Dragons

S tars glisten in the night sky.
P ow! Explosions of colour like a rainbow.
A cross goes a shooting star.
C razy mad-sized planets.
E verywhere you look, there's a planet or a star.

D on't get too close to it; it might burn you alive.
R emember the safety training you went through.
A lthough it will come in handy.
G loopy slime drips on the spaceship.
O n the ship, we start to panic.
N o one was safe from the
S tar-breathing dragon!

Lewis Cameron Breach (8)
Manorfield CE Primary School, Stoney Stanton

The Hands

In my dreams, I wish,
I wish for magical powers,
I set off to search,
I search for the poor,
The poor are sad and cold,
Damp and wet and scared,
Are they going to live?
I don't know, I think I need help,
So I set off to get food,
Meat, fruit, veg,
I need to be quick,
I'm running out of time,
Got the food, need water,
Water from a waterfall,
Quick, ten minutes to spare,
I rushed back and cleaned,
Polished and dusted a few,
All of a sudden,
It happened,
In real life!

Leila Dennis (9)
Manorfield CE Primary School, Stoney Stanton

Proper Horror

As I woke up in this land,
And a drop of rain entered my soul,
My role started to swell,
I could feel nothing but rain,
I stood up, finding a ring,
Where could it lead to?
Hopefully a better world,
Hoping for some luck and hoping for some food,
I put the ring on, then magic smacked my jacket.
I made it so it's worth it,
I travelled to another dimension,
Did I forget to mention,
It got very tragic?
I woke up, only to find a stupid man,
He would try to climb a ladder,
With no climbing wood.

Rihan Stokes (9)
Manorfield CE Primary School, Stoney Stanton

Dinosaurus-Rex

One night I fell into a void,
In a way, kind of like a droid,
I landed in a pot of magic,
But then I did something tragic,
A dinosaur roamed the land,
Now this place wasn't bland,
Then I summoned a tall tower,
After I realised I had power,
I thought I should battle this animal,
But I knew it was a cannibal,
I made a great, sharp sword,
Then the dinosaur roared,
I tried to defeat it with my kicks,
But it had its tricks,
Then I vanished,
I thought I had just been banished.

Jack Siddall (9)
Manorfield CE Primary School, Stoney Stanton

A Footballer's Dream

In my dreams,
A gleaming sun shining,
Bright number fourteen racing,
Through seven people,
There's a referee on the right,
In Leicester City Stadium,
No one can tackle me,
I am unstoppable.

One goal, two goals, three goals, four goals,
I really am unstoppable I am,
With my amazing football friends,
Here are two of them,
One of them is called Lila,
The other one is called Ava.

This ball is obsidian, porcelain,
It is so sleek,
I am so elated and joyful.

Isla Rouse (9)
Manorfield CE Primary School, Stoney Stanton

Pegasus

Dashing through my dreams,
I land in a pile of flashing hay,
Horses neigh, neigh, neighing,
With glittering manes,
And golden coats.
As I realise they're not just horses,
They're pegasi,
With dazzling wings,
And bright manes,
Not just glittering.
When I hop on a horse,
It comforts me as we fly happily.
When we save people from death,
We're mischievous either way,
Thrilled as we come back to Earth,
With his loyalty together,
We make royalty!

Erin Chambers (8)
Manorfield CE Primary School, Stoney Stanton

Favourite Fairies

In my dreams every night,
A fairy shone vividly bright,
Magic appeared from her majestic wings,
How could I breathe from these things?
I can't believe I am helping a fairy,
Even though I'm eating a berry.
As I looked at the iridescent sky,
She decided to pass me by.
I was feeling excited,
Even when I became tempted.
I had an idea that she had friends,
But she sadly did not.
So I went to visit each and every week,
And, phew, I'm back in bed.

Lila Abell (9)
Manorfield CE Primary School, Stoney Stanton

Lost In Monster Woods

Running through the streets, no trees in sight,
Suddenly in a forest, oh what a fright,
The trees are closing in, I don't know what to do,
I'm lost in Monster Woods! Something slimy touches me, boo!
Surrounded by monstrous spiders too!
I'm screaming for help, but there's nothing I can do,
I'm sad, I'm alone, I wish I was with you,
I hope this is just a nightmare,
Someone turn on the light,
Save me from this Monster Wood, save me from this plight.

Eden Jones (10)
Manorfield CE Primary School, Stoney Stanton

In My Room, I Saw A Broom

In my bed, I hurt my head,
I fell asleep and heard a beep.
I saw some trees,
I felt a breeze,
And all of the bees,
Had some peas instead of honey.
I felt a bit giddy and my hands were shaking,
The food was baking.
Bang! Everything burst,
I was so sad,
I felt so bad,
All I had was a broom.
But then, I saw a chocolate and sweet bouncy castle,
Once I saw it, everything was okay,
But still, there was one problem,
I didn't want it.

Eva Rose Major (8)
Manorfield CE Primary School, Stoney Stanton

The Cloaked Man

There was once a man with a cloak,
Whose house was full and dark,
Filled with black smoke.

One day, he went down the stairs,
To see a group of wild bears.

Then, they ran away,
Clearly, they did not want to stay.

Then, he got an axe,
Its name was Max.

He wanted to chop down a tree,
But then he was scared by a bee.

Then, he left the tree,
And so did the bee.

Alfie Beckman (9)
Manorfield CE Primary School, Stoney Stanton

Missing

M ighty spiders crawling around. I don't know why,
I ridescent legs shining brightly in the night sky.
S cared as I run away. Clowns shine brightly in my eyes,
S uspicious why the clowns and spiders are near me.
I n the sunset, I try to go by,
N early the next morning. I now have nightmares.
G etting up, I still feel scared and hope I have no more nightmares.

Millie Cassell (9)
Manorfield CE Primary School, Stoney Stanton

Goalkeeper Dreams

Faraway dreams. My dreams are all about football. I was a goalkeeper, one of the best at diving and saving a lot of footballs. Then, I am the speediest goalkeeper ever. Then I am very happy and excited. But someone, who is a very good player, scored lots of goals. I am nervous because he gets best shooter and best skills. But when me versus the best player it is very hard. But I save it quite a lot. But he scored a lot too.

Noah Smith (9)
Manorfield CE Primary School, Stoney Stanton

The Dragon

In my dreams, a bright red dragon is waving his tail. Their starlit tail flies as they twirl their magical arms around. They pass me while I am looking at the rainbow, sparkling with bright shooting stars.
They have come to Earth to me every night. I leave my bedroom but they follow me on the roof. Maybe jumping will make them stay but sadly they disappear in the sky. Not there, but next year they might come back...

Ronnie Willows (9)
Manorfield CE Primary School, Stoney Stanton

Mythical Adventures

In my scary dreams,
I see a mysterious island but,
If I knew I wouldn't have made it,
This mistake on the haunted island,
There were a tonne of musty skulls,
In the distance, I saw a pirate ship,
Could it be?
I was completely scared and lost if I went back,
There would be big monsters,
I looked and ran, I built a shelter,
While the Greeks invaded.

Artjoms Trifonovs (9)
Manorfield CE Primary School, Stoney Stanton

Mythical Land

A few days ago,
With dragons, skeletons and clowns,
I got sucked into my video game.
I was trying to find shelter,
From the fire-breathing dragons,
And the clowns with horrible faces.
They were trying to get me,
And then I met a talking tree called Groot!
I also met a talking racoon called Rocket!
A wizard called Bob was also there,
I now live there.

Sebby Jones (9)
Manorfield CE Primary School, Stoney Stanton

A Mythical Adventure

In my dreams,
Where there are dark lands,
I fight dragons,
With golden hands,
Which took over my castle,
In my tiny town,
I fight for freedom,
With wizards and dwarves,
Now I'm awake, safe in my bed,
But am I? Oh, no,
There's a monster under my bed,
But look, there's a wizard friend,
Phew, I'm safe now,
Safe in my bed.

Sebastian Wegerif (9)
Manorfield CE Primary School, Stoney Stanton

Volcanoes

A magical place where there are volcanoes.

V olcanoes: there are scary ones, amethyst ones,
O nes that I can't explain,
L arge ones, tall ones and even small ones,
C urly ones, magical ones and dangerous ones,
A magical place no one knows about,
N o one, no human, except me,
O h no! It's erupting.

Lewis Sterland (8)
Manorfield CE Primary School, Stoney Stanton

Ghost Football

I am in my dreams, with a ghost football.
No one can see it, but I can.
It must have magical powers,
Messi and Vardy beside me.
I must be in a dream, but it looks so realistic.
I am happy, but sad this is not real,
It's fake, in a stadium in my head.
But I am still in my bed,
Thrilled and elated that I am with
Messi and Vardy in my head.

Franklin Knight (8)
Manorfield CE Primary School, Stoney Stanton

Football Paradise

In my dreams every night
I dream that I play football
But normally when it ends I wake up
But today it was different
My friends went to a stage with a trophy
But at one moment everyone collapsed
When I woke up I was in paradise
And for a while, we did shooting at a wall
But one moment I woke up for school
"Phew, until next time..."

Max Holmes (9)
Manorfield CE Primary School, Stoney Stanton

My Annoying Friend That I Have Got

I have an annoying friend who always follows me around, even at the shop, even to the bathroom. Even if I lock him out of the house, he will still be in the house. It is really weird. Sometimes he hides under my bed so I can't see him there. I can see you under my bed.
I have no food because every time I buy some, he eats it, then leaves. It is a good time when he leaves.

Alaya Cherry (9)
Manorfield CE Primary School, Stoney Stanton

The Dragon's Tale

Bob, Billy and I saw something soaring through the sky. Stars were shining bright. A twinkle burst from the light, through day and happiness onto the Earth below. In a cage, the Sun Dragon lay and said, "I got trapped by the Moon Dragon!"

Bob stood there, frozen. It was dark and creepy noises rose from the ground. The history of dragons was upon us.

Arrabella Rose Lee-Fowler (9)
Manorfield CE Primary School, Stoney Stanton

The Fallen

1914, thousands and thousands of men walking across the misty and marshy
And bodies and cans, *boom, bang, crash, boom!*
Men dropping like flies
I heard screams and shouting, whistling, *sss!*
A whistle blew, men in cavalry failed to stand their ground.
That I might fail to stand my ground and make my peace without a sound.

Tom Farrell (9)
Manorfield CE Primary School, Stoney Stanton

Football Dreams

Winning the World Cup
In 2026

Nobody can tackle me
Nobody can see me
Neither can my teammates...

Then I arrived at Wembley
I could see the other team
Menacing, ready

They looked at me
I looked at them
They didn't know what to expect
The crowd was chanting my name, I was ready.

Casper White (9)
Manorfield CE Primary School, Stoney Stanton

A Day At Hogwarts

In my dreams,
I get taken to a magical castle,
Where there are dragons,
Famous wizards.
I think I know where I'm at,
I'm not so sure.
I get to a Quidditch court,
With flying brooms everywhere.
Then I meet Harry Potter.
I am filled with excitement.
Then I watch the Quidditch.
I am so happy.

James Pickering (9)
Manorfield CE Primary School, Stoney Stanton

A Vortex To A Different World

In my nightmares,
I get stuck in a hopeless land,
Where no human has ever breathed.

A desperate planet with vast deserts,
The dead biome had no life,
The only thing was a tumbleweed.

I thought I was alone until,
Some sort of creature reared above me,
Then I woke up ready for school, terrified.

James Heptinstall (9)
Manorfield CE Primary School, Stoney Stanton

Where Do They Live?

Dreaming, nightmares,
Where do they live?
In your brain, in your ribs?
They're wonderful things,
Some good, some bad,
Where will you find them?

Where do they live?
Are they mad?
They are in your body,
What do you think they are?

Why do they live in your body?
Why! Why! Why!

Myla Shilcock (8)
Manorfield CE Primary School, Stoney Stanton

Wizards

W aterfalls running by a castle,
I 'm dreaming of a magical world,
Z ooming wizards flying in the sky,
A nd odd creatures sprinting in a forest,
R unning on green grass, I find a,
D ecaying ruin, what do I do?
S omething so fast, it's as blurry as tracing paper.

Kelly Wassell (9)
Manorfield CE Primary School, Stoney Stanton

The Magic Sorcerer

One day, this crazy thing happened. I didn't know what but I was having a bad time with my friend because we were fighting the red and blue. The titans flew. Then, the magic sorcerer flew down from the misty darkness. From the void, we fell into this Lego world. The Lego world that spun and it was dragged into the mist of darkness.

Jacob Grant (9)
Manorfield CE Primary School, Stoney Stanton

The Green World

There was a girl called Bella and she had a world with no plastic. It was quite fantastic. Once she found a hidden door in a tree she wanted to explore the hidden door. She went in the door, and the world was lovely. It was luscious and green. She was in a forest better than she had ever seen, and she stayed there forever.

Ayesha Stratton (9)
Manorfield CE Primary School, Stoney Stanton

Why Does This Happen?

Once upon a time, when I was driving to my school I saw something glowing in the sky. It was a meteor heading directly to my school.
One hour later the meteor hit my school. I was really upset that my school got hit by a meteor. Then the meteor started glowing, then it exploded and I was shocked.

Samuel Savage (9)
Manorfield CE Primary School, Stoney Stanton

All About Dragons

Through a thousand walls,
Ten thousand years,
It was finally here: a dragon,
A golden dragon,
On my shoulder,
It jostled on me,
I put it in my hand,
I touched it,
The scales shocked me. They were so soft,
I put it in a jar. It was so satisfying.

Elliott Booth (9)
Manorfield CE Primary School, Stoney Stanton

The Garden Fairies

I was at the park with my cousin and then we saw a note, with glitter in a little bottle. The note said 'You can turn into a fairy and go to the tree that is next to the beehive and go through the hole'. We did that and there was a leaf fairy and a wood fairy and lots more.

Lily Moulin (9)
Manorfield CE Primary School, Stoney Stanton

My Dream Horse

In my dreams,
With my ice horses, although I'm a little sad because I lost my only Pegasus.
I remember when we used to fly in the moonlight,
All of a sudden *boom!* The ground shook and a glossy,
Sleek figure appeared before me.

Connie Law (9)
Manorfield CE Primary School, Stoney Stanton

Space Dancer

Dancer, Dancer in the sky,
Flying through the beautiful sky in the clouds,
There is a mystery.
I wonder what the mystery is.
In the clouds, the mystery is a fairy
Who is very magical, very smart,
And good-looking.

Isla Rae Warner (9)
Manorfield CE Primary School, Stoney Stanton

Magical Football

A magical football is walking by,
Football walks into the football club,
Football asks where are all the other people and buildings,
Football has a Monster can,
Football rides and says, "Oh, this is cool!"

Rardya Babu (8)
Manorfield CE Primary School, Stoney Stanton

The Dragons Of Red And Blue

The dragon of the blue flew,
The dragon of the red led the dragon of the blue.
Well, the dragon of the red,
Fed the dragon of the blue,
They both slept in Dragon World,
At night, everything is possible.

Evelyn Bostock (9)
Manorfield CE Primary School, Stoney Stanton

Dino Finding

I was in a land full of dinosaurs, which didn't see me. There was a T-rex. I snuck around and found other types of dinosaurs, like a Hipnosaurus, a Pladocus, and a Slipinsaurus. Maybe I should find more.

Delaney Keeler (9)
Manorfield CE Primary School, Stoney Stanton

Dinosaurs Of The Red And Blue!

Red and blue, the dinosaurs formed a plan.
A man had a genius plan to slice and dice these monsters.
The cave they lurked in was filled with redstone and diamonds.
He went in but not out.

Max Chapman (9)
Manorfield CE Primary School, Stoney Stanton

The TMNT

In the sewer there lived four baby turtles
They were green but brighter
It was like a green liquid
I called it ooze
I raised all four of them
They fought crime.

Zachary Blockley (8)
Manorfield CE Primary School, Stoney Stanton

Hell

N othing has prepared me for this, not even words or anything else, all I see is fog!
I walk falling over, catching my foot on roots
G lancing everywhere, making sure clowns are not following me, nothing
H ow on Earth did I get here? Is this a prank? Guys, this is not funny!
T hen I stumble to a house, I go inside and turn the lights on
T urns out it is a devil family, I think one looks like me!
M y worst fear is to be caught by a devil and die!
A nd then a devil comes down with nunchucks, I freeze and stop breathing
R unning once I unfreeze, running into devils everywhere
E verywhere are devil guards as well, I find something that says *Go To Freedom*
S o I go through and I... am home safe in bed.

William English (9)
Redfield Edge Primary School, Bristol

Carolyn

Where am I? What should I do?
All I see is a girl dressed in blue,
She doesn't have a very creepy face,
It is just a very weird place,
Where is she going? She's starting to leap,
All I think of her is just a weird old creep,
All of the stars are now shooting,
Most of the owls are now hooting!
I'm looking up and I can see Mars,
I look back down and I can see cars,
I forgot I had a clover.
Ah! One of the cars knocked me over!
Where am I going? I'm starting to fall,
By my side is a ball,
I think now I'm starting to lean,
Ah! Now I'm beginning to scream!
I'm on the ground, I see my sister,
I have now got a blister,
What, who is this man?
Why won't he get banned?

Penelope Henderson (9)
Redfield Edge Primary School, Bristol

Ghostbusters

G hosts are everywhere, they are dancing in the sky,
H unting ghosts, "I'm going to get you." What, who said that?
O h, it's a ghost, I better run, "Argh!"
S itting in my room while the chessboard is moving,
T *ick-tock*, ghost clock, running out of time, better run,
B ut then the clock stops moving, and it all freezes,
U nder my bed hiding, hearing giggling from the corridor,
S cared as can be, running away,
"T eatime." What, who said that? Mum's not home,
E ating, my food tastes disgusting with slime all over it,
R eject your house if you hear or see anything weird,
S aved the world, killed the ghosts, yeah.

Poppie Palmer (8)
Redfield Edge Primary School, Bristol

Dawn Rises

As dawn rises again,
The townsfolk remember their skills again,
But no one remembers the fun they had,
So this night, I will try to amaze the world.

Even if it means I should go through the hills,
Even if it means I go through the fields,
And go through the valley of heroes once more,
I will always know the way to my home,
Evermore.

I went through the shadowy valley unaware,
I was busy, hunted by the savage bear,
But with one thump and kick,
The heroes appear with a flick.

Help me guide the Evermore stones,
With a crack and thump, I'm nearly dead,
Then I wonder, am I lost from dread?
Will I ever get back?

Ede Turczi Blair (10)
Redfield Edge Primary School, Bristol

The Deadly Waterslide

All of the people went down the slide. Nobody noticed that it was a deadly slide and lots of people had died. They cracked their faces and it was a racket, it was a creepy sight.
I went to the lifeguard; nobody was there. I went to my friends, they were called Lucas and Joshua. We went outside. We saw the creepy thing, it said, "If you come you will die if you go on the slide." It was a deadly surprise, everybody ran away but me and my friends. We wanted to know who was doing this so we were checking the place out. We saw a person with a bag of money, it was a creep. "We follow him," said Joshua. So we did. He went in where nobody was allowed...

James Dheilly (9)
Redfield Edge Primary School, Bristol

Underwater Paradise

Under the water, I go,
Down down I know,
Ain't no surfers above me,
I feel so fluffy,
Underwater paradise before my eyes,
Don't splash or you'll get a surprise,
Next to me Aqua Man,
He doesn't need a tan,
Squint your eyes and you might be able to see,
Swordfish all around me,
Ain't no sharks around,
Because Aqua Man's in town,
When I get to my room,
It's almost noon,
I go to see the flying fish,
I heard one of them is called Trish,
I go to the casino,
And win some like I'm Nemo,
The Aqua Man gets his underwater hound,
To guide me back above ground.

Rowan Haddrell (9)
Redfield Edge Primary School, Bristol

Kangaroo Cakes

My kangaroo and I make a cake at the lake, we bake a Nutella cake.
My loving eyes are glowing like the sun in the sky, making and baking Nutella cakes.
My kangaroo loves cooking but sometimes she's too busy looking at the neighbours cooking.
The flowers were power.
She sometimes gets messy, baking with her friend Nessie,
Most of all my kangaroo likes making cakes, but best of all my kangaroo likes going to parties and eating all the Smarties!

Guess what?
If you hop then you are a kangaroo,
But if you hop and you stop!

There is always time for Nutella cake with Nessie and all your friends around you.

Ava Woodham (9)
Redfield Edge Primary School, Bristol

Me And Dwayne Johnson

Once upon a time, not long ago, me and Dwayne were in the big O. The sea waves went up and down, like a merry-go-round.
All of a sudden, a monster came out of the water, with eyes the size of boulders. When we saw it, we shook to our bones, but then we realised we were all alone.
The monster played, shook and broke our ship. We knew he was making us his fish and chips. I was mad and sad about it, but then God gave me a hint.
Me and big, strong Dwayne made this creature not see the light of day. We hit, shot and beat him, then sat on a bench, sending the creature back to the Mariana Trench.

Jakob Fudge (9)
Redfield Edge Primary School, Bristol

The Somme

I lie in the trench one day to pay the price. I look at the dead men scattered across the battlefield. I hear gunshots whizzing past me and see hand grenades destroying men on the horrible, deadly field. The sound of dying men...
I duck so the shot will miss me, and then I pause and think, *what's the meaning of this war? Is it really just for power? And what is the meaning of life?*
I look back up. I get shot in the head, and I fall to the floor. I scramble up and see that I'm safe, and it has just been a dream.

Ethan Clift (9)
Redfield Edge Primary School, Bristol

The Explorer!

The explorer has come to find a creature,
he has come to take a picture.
Enter the dark cave to find the monster.
Every day, he gets worse and worse.
There are footprints leading into the cave.
The monster gets people to be his slave.
If you see the monster alone,
make sure to not look at your phone,
because the monster can hack into your phone
and you'll be hacked.
So be careful, because you need to be packed.
The explorer is in the cave.
Hopefully he lives.

Sonny Graham (9)
Redfield Edge Primary School, Bristol

Killer Doll

K iller dolls are the worst,
I think you'll see it,
L ooking at me,
L oser, she would scream at my face,
E w, she is very scary,
R un away from home, into the attic.

D oll is hiding, as high as can be,
O ld mirrors shout at me, but not the doll,
L ook, I'm running away,
L ook over there, there is a sign.

I'm now on the ground,
With my sister,
I think I have a blister.

Scarlett Saunders-Rawlings (9)
Redfield Edge Primary School, Bristol

Black Pearl

B ehind me shouts echo all around,
L ike war has sounded,
A ll of a sudden orders from the Captain,
C ackling before me, Davey Jones stands,
K icking and struggling, Will Turner fights.

P eople of the crew help hoist the sails,
E ven Jack Sparrow pulls on the ropes,
A t the top of the deck is Elizabeth Swan,
R ocking the decks is the dead but alive,
L et out a shout and the war has started.

Nevaeh Newland (9)
Redfield Edge Primary School, Bristol

The Nightmare Dream

D ragons surround me as I set foot on stage, a light shines and a,
R oom appears and I walk toward the light, which turns red. Then it says,
"**E** valyn." A voice as light as a feather speaks.
A person appears in front of me... It couldn't be? Could it?
M y oldest friend suddenly moulds into a goblin and I scream as he moulds again into a dragon. "Who are you?" I say. "I am the shape-shifter," he says grimly.

Evalyn Webb (8)
Redfield Edge Primary School, Bristol

Gerald The Giraffe

We dance in the sky,
We look like birds, together we fly.
In the sugar, we bake a cake,
Looking at animals in the lakes.
Such as elephants, lions, meerkats, wild boars and hyenas.
Me and my giraffe bake in a lake, and it's a fantastic vanilla cake!
He loves parties and Smarties,
We feel happy and excited, and guess what,
If you like spots, then you are a giraffe fan!
We see rainbow rivers, the lake is perfect to swim in!

Olivia Saunders (8)
Redfield Edge Primary School, Bristol

Fire Tiger

F ire burns the wood into ashes,
I gnite the fire,
R oars as loud as thunder and lightning crashing through the night,
E nergetic as a lightning bolt,

T igers wander through the colourful rainforest,
I ndependent as can be,
G rowls like a lion king of the jungle,
E legant as a ballet dancer,
R esilient as an ant carrying all of the food.

Sophia Bird (9)
Redfield Edge Primary School, Bristol

Nightfall

N ight falls over my head,
I just wish I was in bed.
G ruesome murderers' guns shooting,
H ighly intelligent pirates stealing.
T errifying bandits scattered away,
M onsters crawling to their prey.
A re you going to die in pain?
R uins of school in a horrid crane,
E yes laid on the floor.
S oon, the poor come to ignore.

Jack Watkins (9)
Redfield Edge Primary School, Bristol

The Escape From Hell

Blood, knives all around me,
I'm in prison, don't you see?
I saw a murderer kill my brother,
I hope he is not any more bad,
What do I do? I am in a cell,
No! What was that? Did someone yell?
Everywhere I look, I can always see a spider,
All I really need is at least one protector,
I keep hearing noises and it's getting colder,
Is someone here? Maybe it's a monster.

Isaac Purvis (8)
Redfield Edge Primary School, Bristol

Olympic Gymnast

It's now my time to shine,
That gold medal will be mine.
Being an Olympic gymnast would be bliss,
I have trained so hard for this!
This has been my lifelong dream,
Flipping off of that high beam.
The bar, the beam, the floor routine,
The crowd goes wild, I can hear them scream!
I am so proud of what I have achieved,
Because I have always believed.

Darcey Lonergan (8)
Redfield Edge Primary School, Bristol

Manhunt

M e: all I can see, as dark as can be
A t the end, I climb over spiders and rats
N ow I'm outside. It's all red like hell, but worse.
H ungry as can be, running home to see
U nder my bed, turning on the TV. A doll crawls out
N ow I'm digging a hole in my garden
T he doll is outside, near me and my shed.

Fynley Burke (9)
Redfield Edge Primary School, Bristol

I Love To Dream

They take us to the unknown,
They can bring fear,
They can bring happiness,
They don't only happen at night,
I can fly,
I can spy,
I can dance,
I can prance,
I love to dream,
They bring me friends,
They bring me love,
They bring me tears,
They make me be whoever I want to be,
Oh, how I love to dream.

Harry Haskins (8)
Redfield Edge Primary School, Bristol

Fortnite

F ortnite is the best game ever,
O f course, I love it!
R eckless Railways, the best place to drop,
T ime to win, let's go!
N o time to waste, let's get geared up!
I 've almost won, one player left,
T ime to get to the next zone,
E veryone cheers, I won, hooray!

Lucas Henley (8)
Redfield Edge Primary School, Bristol

Nightmares

N ighttime is here and
I go to my friend's to
G o to shoot some people. We go
H igh on wings and
T ravel to battle a boss.
M e and my friend Lucas and Harry drop
A nd we see
R eally good players from the
E ast and we finally
S hoot them.

Joshua Moate (8)
Redfield Edge Primary School, Bristol

My Boat

Here I am, on a ship,
The ocean to see,
Me and my crew on the boat,
Sailing out to sea.
So I'm feeling great but cautious about the sea calling me,
Put on my shoes, but I can see an iceberg bowling,
On the ship, the lifeboats are gone,
Do I see another ship? No.

Toby Piotrowski (9)
Redfield Edge Primary School, Bristol

Squishmallow Park

Once upon a time
On the line
I went to a park
Trees dressed in bark
A Squishmallow there
Now they're everywhere
With some guys
Big blue skies
But then a hen
Found a pen
With a bar
A chocolate bar
With a fish
Came a wish
Let's go eat
Just some meat
Now we're alone
Let's go home!

Daniel Bullock (9)
Redfield Edge Primary School, Bristol

Wishes

W onderful places, far away,
I travel to them in my bed,
S o many fairies flying around,
H ardly any monsters about,
E verywhere you look, there are wishes flying,
S ummoning things in the sky.

Isla Anderson (9)
Redfield Edge Primary School, Bristol

Duck

D uck has a flying friend called Apple
U p in the sky they go
C olourful colours in the sky
K arate in the sky.

Josh Moore (9)
Redfield Edge Primary School, Bristol

My Life

When I grow up I want to be a renal doctor. A renal doctor is a doctor who helps people with kidney problems. I want to move out of my parents' house, and have two kids, with three rooms and a second-level house. I want a dog and a beautiful back garden and a front garden. I want my babies' rooms baby pink, as bright as the sun.
I would also like to spend time with my family and work Mondays, Tuesdays and Saturdays. I would help patients when they go for surgeries and their nerves. I want to spend time in my warm, cosy home. I would spoil my children but not too much. I hope to make lots of money to go on holidays with my family. I would like to hang out with some of my friends. I hope to set myself to a higher standard.

Laurie Elizabeth Hastings (9)
St Kevin's Primary School, Bargeddie

A Dream Made For Me

Each time I go to sleep,
I have to count the sheep,
I wake up in a wonderland full of fun things,
Dragons, dinosaurs, dancers and ducks,
In a world full of daisies, I always have good luck.
There's ice cream and icing,
Something's always surprising,
I don't want to return to go to school and learn,
But without my family,
I feel ever so unhappy,
I feel like weeping,
But for now I'll just keep sleeping,
I close my eyes in this fantasy world,
And hope I wake up and everything is not made up.

Phoebe Gregory (9)
St Kevin's Primary School, Bargeddie

The Amazing Game I Went To

One night, when I went to sleep, I saw myself in a football game. The football game was about to start. I was playing striker for Real Madrid.
When I kicked the ball, the game started. I was in shock that I was playing for the best team in the world. Then, when I scored my third goal and got made 'man of the match', I knew I was going to be a legend.

Matthew Atley (9)
St Kevin's Primary School, Bargeddie

One Day....

One day, I woke up in a magical land with ripped clothes, and lots of sand.
I saw lots of steam so I was shocked by what I saw, a big massive team. So I ran for my life, then they said, "Get the laser beam."
I ran with dread, just to realise, I'm cosy in bed.

Oscar Kaney (9)
St Kevin's Primary School, Bargeddie

Pocket Full Of Dreams

Coins that jingle, notes that fold,
Money to spend and so much more,
Everywhere I look treasure shines,
In this dream, all is mine.

I buy toys that I've always craved,
And by wealth, I feel so saved,
I give to those who have not much,
With every single life I touch.

I travel to places far and wide,
With luxury always by my side,
Every wish is my command,
In this rich life, oh so grand.

But even with this wealth to hold,
I know that friends are worth more than gold,
For richness comes in many forms,
Not just in wealth but love that warms.

Ishraj Arora (10)
St Stephen's CE Primary School, Bury

Dream The Night

In the velvet night, where stars gleam,
Dreams dance and twirl in silent flight.
They whisper secrets, woven in moonbeams' stream,
In the realm of slumber, where fantasies teem.

Through the corridors of the mind they stray,
Painting landscapes of another day.
In dreams, we find solace, hope and grace,
A sanctuary from life's frenetic pace.

So close your eyes and dare to believe,
In the magic that dreams alone can weave.
For in their embrace, we're forever free,
To explore the depths of our reality.

Lewis (10)
St Stephen's CE Primary School, Bury

Once Upon The Game You Love

You love the game, with all your heart,
You chased the ball with might,
You ran and kicked and passed and shot,
With skill and speed and fight.

That's why football is my favourite game,
I love to watch them play,
How fluidly and gracefully they dance across the green,
Such elegant contenders play, the best I've ever seen.

Some people think I'm crazy,
The way I love this game,
But I'd rather be watching football,
Than anything else I can name;
Of course, I may be prejudiced.

Ali Bilal (9)
St Stephen's CE Primary School, Bury

Court, Law And Order

In my dreams, a court stands before me. A surge of fear circulates my body as I begin to say my client is innocent while others say otherwise. The jury watches in intriguement as we pull out solid proof while the prosecutors point out my, so-called, mistakes while people behind me are on the edge of their seats, mouths wide open in shock.
After what feels like an eternity, the jury has decided. Filled with fear, I drop to my knees as they find him... guilty! I slump out, filled with dread, feeling like a complete failure. Then I wake up with a cold sweat.

Rob Keegan (9)
St Stephen's CE Primary School, Bury

Fairy Reaper

F lying high through the sky,
A scend into the stars so bright,
I n the night, we will fly,
R unning on the grass,
Y oung children sleeping.

R eady or not, better start hiding,
E ven if you try to run, you won't make it far,
A xes in his hands, here comes the fairy reaper,
P ack up your stuff until he tries to kill ya,
E yes red, glowing in the dark,
R iding on the grass, better watch out, he's as fast as a dart.

Bradley Oscar Todd (10)
St Stephen's CE Primary School, Bury

Nightmare's Embrace: A Journey Through The Shadow

In the depths of night, shadows creep,
A haunting dream, I cannot sleep.
Monsters lurk, their eyes ablaze,
In this twisted maze, my mind's a haze.

Whispers echo, darkness surrounds,
Nightmare's grip, my heart confounds.
Through the abyss, I try to flee,
But the nightmare's grasp won't set me free.

Tangled thoughts, a chilling fright,
In this realm, where day turns to night.
But fear not, my friend, for morning light,
Will banish nightmares with its might...

Sammi Minhas (10)
St Stephen's CE Primary School, Bury

Lost In A Dream

In my dreams,
I was lost in a forest that scared me to death,
It was like I was losing my breath,
As it was dark I looked for light,
Then an eerie shadow caught my sight,
I was frightened,
I screamed and ran up a hill,
Until I noticed it was a chill,
I walked and walked just a bit more until I fell into a hole,
It felt like I had hit a pole,
After a while, I woke up in my bed,
I was all red,
About a few minutes later, I told myself that I was just lost in a dream...

Minahil Iqbal Raza (10)
St Stephen's CE Primary School, Bury

Dinosaurs!

D eep in the jungle, no friend in sight,
I n between all the trees, I got a fright,
N ever would I have expected to see what I saw,
O h my! A giant, scaly dinosaur!
S haking and scared, I began to run,
A ll I could see was a bright, yellow sun,
U nder it a shadow appeared,
"**R** ory's my name and I don't need to be feared!"
S aving the day, he picked me up and flew away.

Archie Hardman (10)
St Stephen's CE Primary School, Bury

Footballer

F rom game to game, I win every day,
O n the field, I see hay,
O ver the years they have to pay,
T ill the end, I'll say yay,
B ut that's not all, I have to pray,
A s I learn new skills every day,
L oving to be better as I play,
L iking not to have a delay,
E specially not to go astray,
R eassured I'll always be a winner today.

Joshua Adegoke (9)
St Stephen's CE Primary School, Bury

The Dream Of A Son

A spectacular view shocked my eyes with joy. Bentley, Bugatti, Ferrari and many more, all my dreams in one. I couldn't believe my eyes, a football-themed car with my very own favourite Cristiano Ronaldo signed car. What amazed me more, I met him. He shook my hand, *wow!* What a dream come true today.
But when I woke up I realised it was all a dream...

Hadi Abdul (9)
St Stephen's CE Primary School, Bury

Spiders!

S illy old spiders were living happily,
P utting webs there like a family,
I had a dream that they were gone,
D oing their jobs but now it was done,
E veryone looked for the creatures but still, they were nowhere to be seen,
R evealing I was not so keen,
S oon I realised it was just a dream.

Holliemae Newton (10)
St Stephen's CE Primary School, Bury

Our Ukraine

Frightened in the black forest
Once I looked around I stepped one step forward
I was holding in my hand coloured pencils
I wanted to paint the Crimean Mountains and the Carpathians
The steppe and hills of the Dnieper lakes
And eyebrows and a rainbow and a viburnum
The Black Sea and the Danube
All this is our Ukraine.

Amir Muhsin (10)
St Stephen's CE Primary School, Bury

Nightmare

It was chilly, I was frozen,
I saw a token,
Which got stolen,
The windows were broken,
My eyes got swollen.

I couldn't see the sun,
I started to run,
I thought I was done,
This night wasn't fun,
I woke up and it was just a nightmare.

Hamda Irfan (10)
St Stephen's CE Primary School, Bury

Perhaps They Will Listen Now...

Vincent van Gogh, starry Starry Night,
Look at my colours, they're so bright,
Look at my sunflowers,
I still don't think I've got many powers,
I didn't realise I told myself a big lie,
And wish now I could never die.

Nathanael Thorne (10)
St Stephen's CE Primary School, Bury

Alien

A liens are from space,
L onely, above the human race,
I wish I could meet one face-to-face,
E very night I dream about going to space,
N ightly I dream about us meeting face-to-face.

Benjamin Ryan (9)
St Stephen's CE Primary School, Bury

YOUNG WRITERS INFORMATION

We hope you have enjoyed reading this book – and that you will continue to in the coming years.

If you're a young writer who enjoys reading and creative writing, or the parent of an enthusiastic poet or story writer, do visit our website **www.youngwriters.co.uk**. Here you will find free competitions, workshops and games, as well as recommended reads, a poetry glossary and our blog.

If you would like to order further copies of this book, or any of our other titles, then please give us a call or visit **www.youngwriters.co.uk**.

Young Writers
Remus House
Coltsfoot Drive
Peterborough
PE2 9BF
(01733) 890066
info@youngwriters.co.uk

YoungWritersUK   **YoungWritersCW**
youngwriterscw   **youngwriterscw**